CITIZEN UNDER SIEGE

G.N. Devy writes in three languages—Marathi, Gujarati and English—and has authored or edited over a hundred works in areas such as Literary Criticism, Education, Linguistics, Anthropology and History. Several of his books have been translated into Marathi, Gujarati, Kannada, Malayalam, Tamil, Telugu, Bangla, Konkani, Hindi and Assamiya. He was formerly Professor of English at the Maharaja Sayajirao University of Baroda, Professor of Humanities at the Dhirubhai Ambani Institute of Information and Communication Technology, Gandhinagar, Professor of Social Sciences at the Centre for Multi-disciplinary Development Research, Dharwad, Obaid Siddiqi Chair Professor at the National Centre for Biological Sciences, Tata Institute of Fundamental Research (TIFR), Bangalore, and is currently Senior Professor of Eminence & Director, Somaiya School of Civilization Studies, Somaiya Vidyavihar University, Mumbai. He founded the Bhasha Research and Publication Centre at Baroda (1996) and Adivasi Academy at Tejgadh (1999). The People's Linguistic Survey of India, covering 780 living languages of India and published in 50 multilingual volumes, was a unique project initiated and led by him. Devy is a thinker, cultural activist and a distinguished academic. He has held several distinguished fellowships and received numerous Lifetime Achievement honours, including the Padma Shri, and awards such as the Sahitya Akademi Award, SAARC Foundation Award, Prince Claus Award and Linguapax Award. He is Senior Honorary Fellow of the Asiatic Society of Mumbai.

CITIZEN UNDER SIEGE

ESSAYS (2014–2025)

G.N. DEVY

WESTLAND
NON·FICTION

WESTLAND
NON·FICTION

Published by Westland Non-Fiction, an imprint of Westland Books, a division of Nasadiya Technologies Private Limited, in 2025

No. 269/2B, First Floor, 'Irai Arul', Vimalraj Street, Nethaji Nagar, Alapakkam Main Road, Maduravoyal, Chennai 600095

Westland, the Westland logo, Westland Non-Fiction and the Westland Non-Fiction logo are the trademarks of Nasadiya Technologies Private Limited, or its affiliates.

Copyright © G.N. Devy, 2025

G.N. Devy asserts the moral right to be identified as the author of this work.

ISBN: 9789371971577

10 9 8 7 6 5 4 3 2 1

The views and opinions expressed in this work are the author's own and the facts are as reported by him, and the publisher is in no way liable for the same.

All rights reserved

Typeset by Mukul

Printed at Parksons Graphics Pvt. Ltd

No part of this book may be reproduced, or stored in a retrieval system, or transmitted in any form or by any means, electronic, mechanical, photocopying, recording, or otherwise, without express written permission of the publisher.

For Surekha

Contents

Acknowledgements ix
Preface xi

The Elusive India 1
Number Games Through the Eyes of Citizens 6
In the Eye of the State 11
Free Thought Assassinated 15
Mobs, Mobiles and Silenced Memory 18
Crime Redefined 23
The Anti-CAA Protest 29
Thinking Citizens 49
Migration and the Post-Democracy State 54
The Present and the Past 59
A March to the Future or a Leap Backward? 63
Going Forward to the Past 70
The Future of the Past 75
The Future of History 80
Past Forward: History, Ideology and the Republic 85
The Bull and the Horse 89
Denial of the Past as Historiography 92
Of Many Heroes 96

Educating India to Return to the Past	101
Anti-Science Regime: An Intelligent Design?	106
Scholars Stand Up for Reason	110
Is India Being Pushed into Knowledge Isolation?	114
The Question of Questioning	119
Questions, What?	123
Restoring Questioning	127
Angry Gods, Angry Mobs	131
Death by Wish	135
People in Ward Number Six	139
Disenfranchising the Poor	143
A Hindi India	148
Language Mix and Paranoia	153
A Return to the Returning of Awards	157
The Return of the Mahabharata	161
Genes Inspected, Hate Word Resurrected	165
Pegasus, Equus and Horse Trading	170
Between *Nakba* and *Nauba*	174
A Father and Three Daughters	178
What Is Staring India in the Face	183
The Mother of Democracy	188
What the Thunder Said	192
Must Every Elephant Cease to Be?	196
The Clash of Human Visions of Reality	201
Living in Two Worlds	205
A Song for India	211
Contrarian Present and the Human Future	215
Towards 2047	220

Acknowledgements

The short essays in this collection were originally written between 2019 and 2024 as contributions to *The Telegraph*, *The Indian Express*, *The Hindu*, *Economic & Political Weekly* and the *Open* magazine. With grateful acknowledgement to these media houses and their editors, this collection is a testament to India's worrisome transformation, unfolding with a ceaseless ferocity, and the response to it by an independent, democratic and critical consciousness.

Preface

In the India of the early 1950s, independence was still a fresh concept. The idea of independence had taken hold of the villages and cities for about half a century before the country became officially free from British rule. The formulation of the Constitution in November 1949 and its adoption by the 'people of India' in January 1950 put a formal stamp of authority on the idea that India was to be a constitutional democracy, governed by the people of India through their representatives. I was born in 1950. It goes without saying that the conversations among the adults in my tiny town that I overheard as a child were suffused with a new awareness about what India was. The primary school I attended suddenly had public rituals signifying to the children that the people of India were 'azad'—free. What was true of my small town was equally true of the half a million villages of India during the 1950s.

Much later, during the concluding years of the twentieth century, I began working with Adivasis living on the border between Gujarat and Maharashtra. As part of my work, I regularly attended meetings and discussions with a large number of Adivasi activists and writers from different states. One of them was Atmaram Rathod—he passed away about two decades ago—from the Banjara community. A rebel in nature, Atmaram was a fantastic storyteller. His stories were usually soaked in biting sarcasm. In one of his surreal stories, set during the time of the Ramayana, an old, idealist freedom fighter (I am masking the identity of the protagonist so as to not offend sensibilities) asks his compatriots, 'If India was in chains, and the chains were broken, surely there must be some bits and pieces of chains that are still lying around. Can you show me some?' Nobody has an answer to this absurd question. He goes to other wise men, and when he gets no answer from them, he moves on to the district collector (government officer), ministers, the Union home minister and finally to the prime minister, whom he had known during the freedom struggle. He faces obstacles when he tries to meet the high and mighty: he cannot take an appointment with a person in power without paying a price. In the process, the idealist loses all his belongings, including some parts of his body—given away as bribe—which had given him his distinct identity. In the end, he is promised an answer on the condition that he proves that he is the freedom fighter he claims to be. Having lost his distinct physical features and, by extension, resemblance to his photo in the national identity-card, he is shown the door. Alas, his question remains unanswered.

In every gathering that Atmaram narrated this story, his audience considered it no more than a humorous, mixed-up folktale. My case was different. As I listened to the story over and over again, the fifty years of my life from 1950 to 2000 started flashing before my eyes. In that half century, my life had taken exactly the same course as that of millions of other lives in India: starvation and struggle in the early phase of life, some measure of contentment in the thirties and a sense of having arrived in the forties. The bank balances varied from individual to individual, but the trajectory was more or less similar, except for some iconic celebrities. It is difficult to say if Indians really had come upon freedom during those five decades, or if they had merely moved from being a vast class of rural poor to a vast middle class. This pushed me to start analysing if India had missed out on something crucial in its transformation from a hoard of princely states to a modern democratic nation.

I first heard the expression 'princely state' mentioned in the small town where I spent the early years of my childhood. The raja was still around; but his presence was restricted to his public appearance on festival-rituals. However, I could see around me people—rich as well as poor—with an acute sense of status, a sentiment pervading India of the medieval feudal times. Obviously, a part of it originated in the stringent caste hierarchy; but a lot of it had nothing to do with caste. This was social status beyond the caste framework—status in relation to power as was then structured. Political leaders and administrators commanded respect, but this was born out of fear than out of genuine appreciation of their mental and personal qualities. The law of the land had made people citizens, but they were still emotionally invested in imagined hierarchies. The Constitution had made all of them equal citizens; yet all of them were part of a society made of members affiliated to one or the other rung of the social ladder. In the decades that followed, one saw this new class of 'rulers' treating the law of the land lightly. The high-octane insult of the Constitution in the form of the Emergency of 1975 was the more visible denial of democratic values. Less visibly, almost as a matter of everyday practice, they started getting bruised, kicked and beaten by the high and the low among the people in power. Sometime in the 1980s, phrases like 'nexus between criminals and politicians' became commonplace. At the same time, the indifference of citizens regarding the protection of constitutional values had become the mood of the nation. With rare exceptions, everyone was in a mad rush to grab and corner opportunities in every field. Hardly did the citizens realise that when they compromised with democratic values, their own rights as citizens were the first casualty. What was gained through a long struggle fought with idealism was being squandered at both ends of the power spectrum—the rulers and the ruled. There were, of course, struggles by groups of people—Adivasis, mill workers, farmers, students, environmentalists and artists. But they did not have the same effect on either public morality or the rulers as the earlier struggle for freedom had.

As half a century flashed before my mind's eye, I wondered if there were some invisible chains at work—apart from the discrimination emerging out of gender, caste and class—which kept people away from claiming their rightful and complete citizenship in the wonderful republic that India had become in the year of my birth. By the time this question started haunting me day and night, I had occasions to visit many other countries in several continents. I had also had the benefit of reading a large amount of literature and philosophy drawn from many ancient and modern cultures and languages. Yet, none of that readymade philosophy, anthropology, literature and political thought helped me understand exactly what or who were keeping Indians from acquiring the traits of complete citizens, despite constitutional guarantees. And why the public institutions and governments apparently designed to support these guarantees were curbing citizens' rights in every possible manner. In other words, though I was literate and knew everything that educated persons are expected to know, I did not have a sufficient grasp of the predatory nature underlying the modern state.

It was in the context of this question that educating myself politically started becoming a strong desire within me. By politics, I do not mean information about politicians, parties and their hunt for power. That is one part of politics; but not the most substantial one. The other and more significant part of it is the relationship between the rulers and the ruled. That I began to be political in itself was a bliss, for most of my peers have gone on in life and beyond without that benefit. I have drawn my understanding of politics from little-known rebels like Atmaram Rathod, from Adivasis, nomadic communities and from the marginalised people whose voice gets rarely heard.

A lot of what I gathered from people as a sensibility got illuminated through my numerous conversations with the thinker Shiv Visvanathan and the writer Mahasweta Devi. Shiv has a theory of freedom firmly rooted in the idea of diversity, and of citizenship as the right to laugh and generate metaphors. He had nothing but contempt for the pompous, self-righteous administrators and for the state pretending to be above every rebuttal, rejoinder and critical comment. He thought of diversity as the ultimate theory of power. Mahasweta Devi's idea of power sprang from people's ability to protest, to tear apart all hypocrisy and to weave a vision of the future beyond the confines of every social straightjacketing. Years later, after I gathered her ashes in Kolkata and laid them at the spot in the Adivasi Academy at Tejgadh, where she had desired that she breathe her last, I inscribed her thoughtful sentence: 'Every dream has the right to live.'

Both Mahasweta and Shiv understood what freedom is; and both wrote relentlessly. Shiv did so in a language of riddles and metaphors, Mahasweta in an idiom of creative imagination. I learnt from them how to look at people as primary and the nation as the resulting super-structure, unlike most of my middle-class friends who half-wittedly thought that the state was the nation. My altered understanding of India provided me great sustenance when I got deeper in my work with the nomads, tribals and the marginalised. This understanding became most useful as a theory of language when I launched a nation-wide survey and documentation of the hundreds of languages that India still has; sadly, most of them are labelled dialects. But, most of all, it provided me an inner strength when I decided to openly counter the rise of fascism about a decade ago.

Currently living in the eighth decade of my life, I am acutely aware that the freedom struggle in the first half of the twentieth century succeeded in making India free of the British rule. Yet, so many other fears are instilled among people, and so much intimidation surrounds all of us. Ask an ordinary citizen if the judiciary or the police can provide sufficient protection to women, the oppressed classes and to children when the need for such protection arises. Ask a citizen if, on sensing some grave wrong to an individual or the society, they can hope to be able to stall it. When you spot a wounded or dying person on a roadside, you do not stop by to help in apprehension of protracted legal proceedings and police harassment afterwards. Though we do not articulate it so often, almost all of us constantly live under fear. Worse still is the disillusionment with the state's willingness and ability to bring justice to those who get wronged in every walk of life. Such a population, living constantly under the fear of backlash from the *system*, can hardly sustain a democracy. Sooner or later, it was bound to succumb to the whims of an autocratic leader. We have witnessed it happening. The emergence of fascism in India is founded in a large measure upon the perpetually terrified citizenry. Despite the guarantees given in the Constitution, arrogance of the powerful and fear in the minds of citizens are by now entirely normalised and have become the substratum of the psyche of contemporary Indians. If people see no hope, why will they show a sense of responsibility towards bringing about a change?

The other source of fear is jingoism in the name of religion. Spirituality is one thing. Its universal value lies in keeping humans from behaving like mere animals. So is the case with religious philosophy or metaphysics, as they shape one's world views. But aggressive promotion of religion in secular public spaces and making this aggression the hallmark of a political ideology is nothing but a threat of intimidation and a call for submission. When citizens internalise fear as a form of nationalism, imposing fascist ideologies becomes as easy as planting poisonous weeds on a marshy land.

Last year, as I was reading excerpts from Alexei Navalny's prison diary, published by an American newspaper after his tragic death in Vladimir Putin's Russia, my thoughts turned to the thousands of Russians who came out to pay their last respects to him in biting cold winter. They knew that a silent last bow was the most they could do for him. *The New Yorker*, which published his prison diaries, stated, 'It's impossible to read Navalny's prison diary without being outraged by the tragedy of his suffering, and by his death, in February, in a prison camp north of the Arctic Circle. Yet, again and again, we read an exhortation to live bravely in the face of cruelty. "Don't be afraid of anything," Navalny insists. "This is our country and it's the only one we have."' A brave leader, indeed, with a few thousand fearless followers. But the picture is complete only with the several million who stayed back inside their homes. India is no different. During the last ten years, many writers, thinkers, journalists and public intellectuals got killed here. Thousands of Muslims became victims of hatred and lost their lives in Gujarat. Even earlier, thousands of Sikhs were butchered in blind anger in Delhi. Add to this the long list of farmers' suicides, indiscriminate killings of tribals, gang rapes and atrocities on women in Manipur. Some Indians protested in response to these, a few thousands supported the protest, but millions stayed silent. Even more accepted rape and butchery as normal. Some sick minds even justified the violence and humiliation. Were these people actively consenting to the mindless violence around them? Were they so morally degraded and emotionally bankrupt as to not utter a word against such barbaric acts? Were they simply inhumane, or were they brutalised under the impact of ideologically loaded propaganda? I think these people did indeed fail as human beings, but their primary failure lay in their inadequacy as citizens. To be human is individual; to be a citizen is social. Fearlessness and the clear expression of it make a person a citizen. No democracy can stay alive unless the 'demos' compels the state to provide them the space to become complete citizens. This is not merely about the right to pay taxes and access the benefits the state provides. The state is not just a political and economic arrangement. The 'nation' is not just a transactional contract between those who inhabit it and those who govern it. It is also a moral contract, where people have the obligation to be complete and fearless citizens, and governments have the obligation to enable citizens to live without fear.

Political parties the world over vie to create some form of fear in the minds of voters, primarily to gain power. During my youth, while I was studying in England, I noted that an imagined fear of attack by the then USSR was part of the election campaign. I found it laughable. The USA waged a whole war based on the fear of weapons of mass destruction supposedly hoarded by Saddam Hussein in Iraq. American voters were deeply influenced by this fear. The 'military inspectors' sent to Iraq by the USA to unearth those weapons returned with empty hands. All that it resulted in was mindless destruction and a great human tragedy. In our part of the world too, we have witnessed such irrational fears being invoked—religion portrayed as being under threat; fears of internal disruption from a vague 'foreign hand'; the branding of public intellectuals as 'anti-national'; and the labelling of those criticising the government as the 'tukde-tukde gang' or the gang causing disintegration of India.

In 2016, I moved out of Baroda, where I had spent thirty-five years of academic and social life, and took residence at Dharwad in Karnataka. A year had passed since Comrade Pansare and Dr M.M. Kalburgi were murdered for expressing their views on history and religion. Earlier, Dr Dabholkar had been killed in Pune. In shifting to Dharwad, I wanted to bring together writers and thinkers, and build a sustained resistance to this reign of terror. Dharwad was where Dr Kalburgi spent his working life, and it was here he was murdered. While I was working towards the mobilisation of Indian intellectuals, the Kannada journalist Gauri Lankesh got killed, in 2017. She was a fearless journalist. The killings did not stop there. Many other media persons were detained, imprisoned or eliminated.

Most others were silenced or gagged, either through mere intimidation or through corporate takeover of their papers and TV channels. That story is well-known.

It was at this stage that I was asked by *The Telegraph* to write a regular column for them. Since I had not written much for newspapers before, I hesitated. However, I knew that *The Telegraph* was a courageous publication. Besides, I was assured that I could write on just about any subject I wanted without any editorial interference. When I started the column in 2018, I decided to write around the question of what it means to be a citizen, the pressures faced by Indian citizens and the way they articulate their views. In short, I would write on the politics of Indian citizens. In December 2019 came the Citizenship Amendment Act (CAA), which severely dented the idea of citizen as laid down in the Constitution. A couple of months before the CAA Bill was passed in the Parliament, I had organised a large meeting of representatives from diverse communities and states in Dharwad to think of strategies to resist the impending calamity. Later, after the Bill became an Act, a nationwide protest started. Some of the articles in this book deal with that movement. Many other pieces deal with education policy and the tendency to glorify the past to create a false sense of pride.

When I was fifteen years old and a first-year college student in Pune, I came across a remarkable book of essays. It was a Marathi translation of Arthur Koestler's *The Yogi and the Commissar* by D.N. Shikhare. As a young student hungry for knowledge about the world, I read and re-read it several times. In that remarkable book, Koestler had brought together his writings that had appeared in various British newspapers about the rise of Hitler and Mussolini, their impact on the world and the resistance put up by democratic countries to the threat posed by fascism. Over the six decades since then, I have realised that many of my views echo Keostler's anti-fascist ideas. Encouraged by his example, I felt that some of the essays I had written for *The Telegraph* and *The Indian Express* could be brought together to form a little book. The essay 'Cyber-space Freedom' was written for *Open* magazine and 'Understanding the CAA' appeared in the *Economic & Political Weekly*. In these essays, I look at how the idea of 'citizen' is getting assailed in the name of religion, nation, history and knowledge. Unlike my other books, this is not a sustained thesis on any of these themes, simply because the form of writing I had adopted was not conducive for presenting any ponderous thesis. Many of the essays may look topical. Indeed they are; and I have not made any attempt to mask their original purpose and place. I like to hope that they point to a long-term concern and sustained reflection on questions central to the existence and future of the Indian people: Can the besieged Indians regain and protect their space as citizens, the space originally visualised for them in the Constitution? Can democracy as a form of government survive if citizens are kept under fear and surveillance by the state? These questions have gained urgency not just in India but in most countries across the world.

G.N. Devy
Dharwad, Dasara
2025

The Elusive India

There is no dearth of scholarly books on India. The sheer wealth of books in sociology, history, politics, ethnography, culture, religion, philosophy and the mythology in India can easily overwhelm any major library in the world. There is an equally amazing range of creative writing in Indian languages describing Indian people, their emotions, aspirations, experiences, perceptions, dreams and disappointments. Besides, there is quite an ocean of oral compositions and oral traditions that provide us glimpses of Indian society in the past. Yet, not a single work can be considered a comprehensively representative work on India. No single analysis or commentary can be singled out to give a complete picture of India. Whatever one states as the truth of India almost always has a complete opposite standpoint that is equally true. A claim that Indians are brought up on great spiritual traditions is challenged by evidence of their limitless materialism. It is supposed that Indians lack historical sensitivity, but they recall with great precision their kula, gotra, caste laws, myths, legends, centuries-old folklore, village boundaries, pedigree of animals, peculiarities of trees and plant species and, of course, insults meted out to their forefathers by relatives. One often thinks of them as being indifferent to filth in public places, and the misery of the old and the poor. Yet, Indians take personal hygiene and punctually washing their bodies very seriously. They can also be compassionate with complete strangers. Whatever you say about India is just as true as its exact opposite.

What is it about Indians that defies any precise description? What is it about this culture, so often described as a vast, sprawling banyan tree, that bewitches the observer? In Shankara's philosophy of the 'brahm', he proposed a 'never possible to assert'—*na-iti, na-iti, na-iti* (not this, not this, not this)—definition of the invisible but all-encompassing essence. One may find this classical method quite useful as a descriptive strategy to define India. Yet, a much better descriptive strategy would be, perhaps, the exact opposite—to assert all, by saying 'Yes, this, and this too, and this as well' endlessly. About half a century ago, sociologist M.N. Srinivas proposed 'Sanskritisation' as the driving principle of social dynamics in India. He was pointing to the tremendous craving that Indians have towards enhancing their social status—as different from their economic status—particularly within the caste hierarchy. At that time, the Srinivas principle looked like a near perfect depiction of Indian society. But, if one were to look at the numerous agitations demanding an SC or ST status over the last seven decades by communities and castes that were not included in the two schedules, one may conclude with equal ease that 'tribalisation' is as powerful a drive as 'Sanskritisation' in India's social dynamics. Also, the language movements and literary trends that changed the literary sensibility in Marathi, Kannada, Tamil, Hindi and Telugu over those decades point to a craving for 'Prakritisation' rather than 'Sanskritisation' (if one were to take the term literally). In sum, what is true of India is only as much true as its exact opposite.

The struggle for women's rights in India pioneered by Savitribai Phule in the nineteenth century is one of the most glorious pages of its history. Contemporary women in India have come a long way from where they were during the oppressive patriarchal society of ancient India. The days of widow burning and compulsory shaving of heads is a story (indeed a shameful one at that) of the past. Yet, the number of school dropouts among girls has remained the same. The rituals of 'chhat' and 'savitri pooja' that perpetuate women's slavery show no signs of decline. In fact, they are a popular trend of the day. The phrase 'missing women' brought into circulation by Amartya Sen is even now the unmistakable characteristic of India's sociology. What describes the truth of Indian women better—'inhuman oppression' or 'empowering emancipation'? Or is the paradox to be brushed aside by calling it a work in progress?

Indians like to travel. While many migrate out of compulsion, others do so for professional advancement. The global expansion of the Indian diaspora has been unprecedented. One finds Indians in practically every country, big or small. Yet, the peculiar nostalgia that Indians have for their places of origin is phenomenal. Migrants from East Europe residing in mainland western European countries or European settlers in North America are not seen returning to their 'native' locations on a yearly pilgrimage. Indians invariably do, at whatever cost, with the rare exception of the COVID-19 pandemic years. Weddings in India are now scheduled to match the availability of flights from Yorkshire or New Jersey. One wonders, does migration not uproot people from their original places? In the case of Indians, it does not seem to do so, unlike for people from Africa, Latin America or Eastern Europe.

Now let us turn to the most complex question—the nature of urbanisation. In the first place, it is almost impossible to say if India is a predominantly rural and agricultural country, or if it is an urbanised and industrial nation. For one thing, we are highly adept in the art of carrying our rural environ to the city, such that every tier-two city appears to be a sum of numerous villages. At the same time, when visiting a village, one is often surprised at seeing how attached villagers are to whatever city-like gadgets they can get. I am not sure if accurate national data on motorbikes is available; but I shall not be surprised if such data reveals that the number of motorbikes in rural India is many times higher than their number in urban spaces. In a few years' time, the same will happen with four-wheelers. So, does this make the case for a rapidly changing nation? The answer is—clearly, no. The villages have continued to be what they were before. Indian castes and tribes have not changed. Indians—at home or abroad—have not changed much over the centuries. The truth is that we do not know exactly what they have been as villages, people and the society. Thinking and talking about India is indeed an exasperating task.

For one, India is the name for what is inside us—the wealth of our interior spaces—just as it is the name of a people and their nation. That name is essentially plural, though the universal grammar thinks of it as singular. India is India because of its variations and not because of its steadfast unity. The Constitution of India hit the nail on the head when it defined India as 'a Union of States'. It is the union or perhaps a complex co-existence of multiple historical epochs, sensibilities and world views. Every attempt at reducing it to a single track of narrative, order or analysis is likely to end in a frustrating realisation that the exact opposite of that narrative, order or analysis is equally valid. Therefore, if India has to continue being India, it should resist being spoken of as singular.

The acceptance of the diversity, contradictions, surprises and enigmas that India holds before any careful observer, calls for what philosophers describe as 'realism'. That the sociological, linguistic and cultural phenomenon that India is has existed, exists and will continue to exist beyond any individual is the humble realisation that India demands from anyone who inhabits it.

It is no country for egotists, no place for those who think they can clasp it and make it subservient to their view of life. India remains free, for it humbles every egotist. The India that is a complex, beautiful product of its past.

Number Games Through the Eyes of Citizens

THOUSANDS OF YEARS AGO, THE WORD USED FOR '1' WAS 'oynos'. It continued to be in use for nearly three millennia in Indo-European languages until it first became 'oinos' and later 'unus' in Old Latin. Subsequently, in Spanish and Italian, it settled down as 'uno'. One may find the journey of the number through the millennia quite intriguing, particularly through those centuries when humans had not invented number systems or writing to represent thought. Is the ability to count independent of any invented or culturally designed system of numbers? This was a question that fascinated modern cognitive sciences for decades. The currently accepted theory to explain the enigma comes from psychology. The twentieth-century philosopher Jacques Lacan proposed in *Ecrits* that during the cognitive growth of a child between the ages of eight and eighteen months, the infant's brain acquires the ability to distinguish between the self and the other, between oneself and the rest of the world. He also pointed out that it is at this stage that the infant starts looking at oneself through the eyes of others. In order to simplify the concept, Lacan used the example of a child looking at its mirror image— an imagined true presence of itself. To be 'one', as against the externally perceived 'other', has been a primordial psychic drive in humans. Likewise, to be the 'uno', the first among the 'rest', has been an infantile urge in the human psyche; and fulfilling this urge has been characteristic of every egotistic ruler in history.

When I decided to carry out a countrywide survey of languages in India, I thought it would be useful to collect words for numbers in all languages, including those that exist only as oral traditions. It was a fascinating learning experience to go through sets of number-words in over seven hundred languages. Even where communities had forgotten most words in their native languages, the words for the first four numbers were still in existence. I am yet to formulate the theoretical basis for this phenomenon; but my crude understanding is that irrespective of whether language is used and irrespective of whether the language has a script, the human-animal has the innate cognitive ability to formulate a mental image of the outside world. In order to form the image, the ability to conceptualise directions is a prerequisite. On the basis of linguistic evidence, one can conclude that the human brain has a natural capacity to identify and describe—with a fair degree of accuracy—the world outside one's consciousness. In philosophy, this outside world is described as 'reality', not to be confused with Truth, which is a mental judgement. I conclude that the human brain is sufficiently evolved to perceive reality, including the ability to recognise when a false claim to being numero uno tries to hide the 'minus one factor'.

I found corroboration for this hypothesis from an unexpected quarter two decades ago. In those years I was working with Adivasis in Gujarat, which required me to travel a few hundred kilometres to their villages every day. During my travel, I would see a number of large hoardings declaring the allocation of several thousand crores for Adivasi welfare. The larger part of the hoardings was occupied by the image of the then chief minister in a saffron jacket. The figure indicated in the hoarding was exponentially larger than any other allocation in the history of the state. I tried my best going through the state budget to see if the figure aligned with the actual provision. Contrary to my assumption, it did, but only when the allocation for roads, electricity poles, salaries for school teachers, health and irrigation was added to it. When the other allocations were removed, what remained for the poor Adivasis was substantially less than the allocations in previous years. One day, as I stopped by a tea-stall for a cup of tea, I heard a group of young migrant tribals discussing the poster. One of them said, 'The murti (literally 'statue', but here 'image') looks too large.' I was amazed that Adivasis, who would have no way of understanding budget manipulation, had nevertheless grasped the element of deception in it, albeit figuratively.

Years later, the memory of this overheard conversation came back to me when the man who had been the CM of Gujarat appeared on TV [as the Prime Minister] to tell the nation that in 2020, India would allocate 20 lakh crores rupees—a full 10 per cent of the country's GDP—to lift up the sinking economy. Like many other devoted citizens, my eyes filled with gratitude for the generosity of the regime. My tears were also caused by my concern for the migrant workers, entirely overlooked by the state, who might have found the 'murti too large'. This time though, the reaction was immediate. Not just social media 'digitzens', but even international rating agencies and the stock markets were quick to point out that the numbers did not add. Their calculations showed that the promised stimulus veered close to 1 per cent of the GDP. However, was this gross mismatch between the claim and the deed any surprise? It certainly was not, as were the claims of flattening of the curve, the doubling rate of COVID-19 patients, buses and trains being provided for bringing migrant populations home, and train fares of workers being paid by the government. As psychology tells us, the infantile drive to be the numero uno is completely unmindful of the human ability to construct a fairly accurate image of reality.

This brings me to a celebrated short film titled $2 \times 2 = 5$. The film begins by showing a classroom filled with students waiting for their teacher. As he enters, the teacher tells the students that the head teacher was about to make an important announcement. Immediately, the head teacher's voice, brought to the students through a microphone fitted in the room, tells them to follow what the teacher teaches and not to misbehave. The teacher writes on the board—'$2 \times 2 = 5$'. One of the students raises his hand and says, 'But it should be 4.' The teacher barely spares him a look before calling in two senior boys waiting outside the classroom. They step in, pull out their guns and shoot the boy. His blood splatters on the blackboard. The teacher wipes the blood with the duster and continues—'$2 \times 2 = 5$'. The students copy it onto their notebooks. However, one student initially copies what the teacher wrote, but on second thought, strikes out '5' and writes '4' in its place. The film ends there.

Ever since the coronavirus became the media's 'exclusive' topic, there has been a lot of discussion about competing mathematical models, statistical methods, datasets and numbers issued by various authorities and non-government agencies. Questions about data authenticity are repeatedly being raised. And rightly so, if we believe we are still part of a democratic system. However, here is a much graver question—Why has the infantile drive of showing itself off as numero uno found such pervasive space in the government's handling of the people of India? Is this the government's way of concealing from the entire country its own realisation of 'being the second'? Is it a deep-rooted complex of being neglected and defeated in the distant past? Does it not see the obvious, that more and more citizens are likely, speaking in terms of the cinematic representation, to scratch out 5 and write 4 in its place? This ability has been gifted to humans by nature. Can regimes, however self-engrossed, ever reverse it?

In the Eye of the State

Heinrich Heine, one of the greatest German writers of all time, has a frighteningly memorable line to his credit—*'Das war ein Vorspiel nur, dort wo man Bücher verbrennt, verbrennt man am Ende auch Menschen'* ('This was only a prelude; where they burn books, they will ultimately burn people as well'). He was among the other German writers—Maria Remarque, Karl Marx, Albert Einstein and several others—whose books were publicly burnt in May 1933 by the Nazi Students' Association, the SS and the Hitler Youth. They burnt at the Babelplatz in Berlin some twenty thousand books because they promoted ideologies and ideas not acceptable to the Nazis. Heine's quote was a reaction to this ghastly act.

During Joseph Stalin's regime, Aleksandr Solzhenitsyn was charged with 'founding a hostile organisation' and put in the Lubyanka jail. This was in February 1945, just before the Second World War was to end. He had to watch the victory celebration of the war in which he had participated as a soldier and risked his life, from behind the muzzle of the window of his prison cell. Later, he was sent to an isolated prison, the experience that formed the subject of his celebrated work *The Gulag Archipelago*. He was one of the most illustrious of the countless writers who had been imprisoned and tortured for writing what they had witnessed.

Autocratic regimes, whether Right or Left, are hostile to any kind of criticism, and have invariably shown utter disregard for dissenting voices. Of course, this by itself is not the defining feature of such regimes; but it certainly is one of their definitive characteristics. If we look at our own treatment of dissenting voices, we cannot claim a moral high ground. That most of us have forgotten the recent killings of journalists and writers in our country does not mean our report card is free of bloodstains.

Here is a list of people who got killed because they worked with words: 2014: Tarun Kumar Acharya, M.V.N. Shankar; 2015: Jagendra Singh, Sandeep Kothari, Sanjay Pathak, Hemant Yadav; 2016: Karun Misra, Rajdev Ranjan, Kishore Dave; 2017: Gauri Lankesh, Santanu Bhowmik, Sudip Datta Bhowmik; 2018: Navin Nishchal, Shujaat Bukhari, Muhammad Sohail Khan, Chandan Tiwari. The states where these murders occurred include Odisha, Andhra Pradesh, Madhya Pradesh, Uttar Pradesh, Bihar, Gujarat, Karnataka, Tripura and Kashmir. The list would be much longer if one were to include the murders of rationalists like Govind Pansare and M.M. Kalburgi. And even longer if the names of butchered political workers are added. The question here is not who killed them or how, it is why. The timeless, well-known answer for this question is that they were saying things that were inconvenient for the rulers, that their thoughts were seen as 'dangerous'. Sadly, none of the murders generated the censure or public debate they deserved. They were shrugged off as ordinary murders requiring ordinary police enquiries that would inevitably end in dusty files becoming dustier, while the agony of the families of victims grows dull and eventually fades into the forest of cynicism.

This is by no means a uniquely Indian phenomenon. The situation in Russia, China, Turkey, Brazil, East European countries and Bangladesh is no different. Even the United States of America, a country that had firmly advocated for freedom of expression during the Cold War years, has played its own part in the suppression of media; and Trump's presidency has only made things worse. Though the news of explosives dispatched to the CNN office a few years ago did not find headlines in our media, it did send shockwaves in US media circles.

What has changed so radically in the world in recent years? There is, of course, no easy answer; and any attempt to make an objective observation is hindered by the fact that we are currently living through this new era. Yet, I venture to offer a comment, since I find the silencing of dissent and intellectual opposition through violence unacceptable in a civilised society. A rather obvious explanation for the growing intolerance in the world is that during the last three decades, the world has slowly shifted from the distributive-economic model for elimination of inequalities—traditionally held sacred by Left-oriented regimes and social welfare states—to an aspirational-growth model promoted by conservative political parties and Right-oriented states.

With this shift from Left-oriented economic views to Right-oriented economic views, the people in these nations have also gradually gravitated towards the political Right, which in Adolf Hitler's classic (read infamous) formulation, believes that 'the society is like a woman who likes to be tamed and mastered by a strong and powerful leader'. In the last few years, the era of the perceived strong and masterly leader has unfolded in most parts of the world; and, together with the clemency towards violence-prone political regimes, nations have started tolerating extreme Right political parties. In the parliamentary elections held in April 2019 in Spain, nearly one-tenth of the elected members were from the ultra-Right. On 27 April 2019—celebrated in Italy as 'liberation day' since 1945—the Italian ultra-Right took out a parade in Milan, and saluted banners showing Mussolini in real fascist style. In Sweden, France, Germany, Spain, Italy and, of course, Austria, the rise of the ultra-Right during the last few years has served to kindle the hopes of fascist elements. How Europe will cope with the ultra-Right and manage to safeguard its legacy of democracy is not our urgent concern. What matters for us in India is to determine if a transition from our Left economic orientation to the growing aspiration based-model of development can be negotiated without allowing anti–democratic sentiment to rule our heads and hearts.

The destruction of the bust of Ishwarchandra Vidyasagar in Kolkata on 15 May 2019 was a clear indication of how intolerance towards diverse ideas and dissent is taking hold of our minds. It is a testament to how our changing economic wisdom has substantially altered and occluded our idea of democracy. A number of significant changes in Indian history began in Bengal: the Indian renaissance that brought India to the threshold of modernity during the nineteenth century; the rise of the influential middle class towards the end of that century; the rise of the extreme Left in the 1960s; the great decline of Left politics at the beginning of the present century; and most recently, the rise and the mainstreaming of the Right and its doctrine of violence, as symbolised by the destruction of the Vidyasagar statue. May 2019 will continue to engage future historians for a long time. It seems like a good time to read Heine again.

Free Thought Assassinated

It is a common adage that delayed justice is denial of justice. We also know that the Indian judiciary is overburdened by backlog and therefore cannot but be slow. Yet, not all instances of denial of justice can be attributed to judicial lethargy. In the case of many serious crimes, it is the deliberate obstruction by the executive that pushes investigations into blackholes. The criminals involved in the murders of several thinkers in recent years have been roaming free because the police investigation of these cases appear to have been blocked by the government. Though it is difficult to establish this charge by pointing to any acts of commission, the inordinate delay in completing the investigation indicates such a possibility.

Political assassinations of thinkers and leaders are not a new phenomenon. However, during the last few years, India has seen a spate of 'murders of ideological adversaries. Dr Narendra Dabholkar was killed in Pune in 2013, Comrade Govind Pansare in Kolhapur in early 2015, Dr M.M. Kalburgi in Dharwad later that year and Ms Gauri Lankesh in Bangalore in 2017. These were unlike any murders executed by criminal gangs or over petty politics. The victims in all four cases were well-known thinkers and social activists. Their murders show a common method, and going by media reports, a common organisation or individual responsible for their planning and execution through trained attackers. The SIT in Maharashtra and the CID in Karnataka, monitored by their respective high courts, were assigned to investigate these cases. While it is true that the police have arrested various individuals, and in the case of Dr Dabholkar, Dr Kalburgi and Gauri Lankesh, the arrested individuals have admitted to the charges, the masterminds behind the murders remain untouched.

These murders remind one of Ehsan Jafri's murder in Ahmedabad during the 2002 Gujarat riots. In most cases related to the Gujarat riots, investigations were carried out such that the courts had to pass verdicts stating 'not enough evidence to prove' either conspiracy or the crime itself. In several high-profile cases, judges recused themselves; and in one instance, the judge Loya was found dead under mysterious circumstances. Then, in June 2021, journalist Sulabh Srivastava was assaulted to death. If some were murdered, many more were put in prison. There can be a long list of the names of thinkers, activists and dissenters who were jailed because their thoughts did not sync with those of the government. The provisions of the draconian Unlawful Activities Prevention Act (UAPA) are used to back a majority of such arrests. What do these murders and arrests, and the denial of justice to the victims indicate? The cliché often used by those critical of the government is 'an undeclared emergency'. However, it does not provide enough explanation for the phenomenon that has been unfolding in India over the last few years. To understand it, one needs to examine a wide spectrum of acts and utterances. This spectrum includes—but is not limited to—using a troll army to ridicule opponents; intimidation and silencing of media persons by pressurising their employers; blocking of TV channels; mobilisation of vandals to threaten cinema artists; political speeches describing minorities by their food habits and attire to mark them out as 'the other'; labelling every dissenter as 'anti-national'; getting publishers to withdraw books that are critical of the regime; arrests of cartoonists, bloggers and social media users; suspending social media accounts of opposition leaders; snooping on judges, leaders, bureaucrats and citizens; instigator commands like '*goli maaron saalon ko*' given to one's followers; and use of the Enforcement Directorate and CBI to intimidate MLAs and MPs. All these actions need to be seen as expressions of a single emotion—'scorn'—and a single mood—'intolerance'.

Since 2014, scorn and intolerance in public life have raised their ugly hoods. The poison of hatred is spread through WhatsApp messages fed daily to gullible citizens. Intolerance, hatred, scorn, intimidation and violent crimes are a result of the hubris that distinguishes the current regime. The ancient wisdom of the Upanishads taught us to be peace-loving and compassionate. The Constitution which is the very foundation of modern India asks us to respect the freedom of expression. Neither appears to be popular with those in power. Had they been so, the killers of Dabholkar, Pansare, Kalburgi and Gauri Lankesh would have been behind bars by now, and the champions of free thought out of their prison cells.

Mobs, Mobiles and Silenced Memory

T̲HE WORD 'MOB' APPEARED IN THE ENGLISH LANGUAGE towards the end of the seventeenth century. Initially, it was used as a synonym for so many diverse words that in comparison, the contemporary term 'post-truth' appears to be the epitome of semantic lucidity. Following the French Revolution and throughout the nineteenth century, the term 'mob' expressed ultimate social contempt. Half a century passed before the human side of the undifferentiated crowd started receiving attention. This happened when the term 'mobilisation' — in the positive sense — as the first step towards revolutionary changes found its place in political discourse. However, a more compassionate view of the 'mob' emerged when the 'mobile', originally meaning 'mechanical', came in circulation as its complement. If mobs were human, then 'mobile' — though moving — was mechanical. Even when the 'mobile' was not entirely intended to be a machine-driven car but a work of 'kinetic art', it was the mechanical side that was being highlighted. Mobs and mobiles were indeed at odds throughout the twentieth century; but they both remained at the centre of modern history, with revolutions where mobs played a great role or the industrial revolution in which the mobile-steel was crucial. Mobility—human or machine driven—has indeed been at the heart of modernity.

Mobs of the twentieth century were regarded as people who lacked social or cultural memory. They were neither rich, nor upper-caste, nor aristocrats. The earliest mobiles, created in the furnace of the Industrial Revolution, had no memory to speak of. But memory is not to the brain what a limb is to the body—an integral part. It is an acquisition in the process of human evolution; and by the end of the twentieth century, the homo sapiens decided, tacitly though collectively, that the task of processing, storing and retrieving memory at will is not worthy of human labour. They began outsourcing this tedious work to intelligent machines and artificial chips. While chips held memory, mobiles became the repositories of chips. Mobs, shorn of the memory of struggles they had waged for over a century for freedom, equality, dignity and rights, started behaving more like what mobiles had been. Mobiles, on the other hand, aspired to become mobs. The two together are reshaping human memory. For homo sapiens of the twenty-first century, memory is of no great use. All they are excited about is the future. They derive happiness from the wellness of their credit cards which enable them to make purchases from their future earnings. Their relationship with the earth is based on exploiting resources meant for the future. They are not interested in looking back at how long they have lived, and instead focus on how much longer they will. This new species in becoming, described in terms like 'cyborgs' and 'homo dues', does not care much for memory. Memory, they irresponsibly assume, mobiles can do, much like how Bohemian artists thought, 'living, that the servants can do'. Memory, as it were, is no longer of value to humans. Mobiles, the multi-tasked tablets, on their part, hold a tantalising vision before us. They can buy and sell things for us, convey sentiments for us, open up universes stranger than humans have ever known, freeze time in photo-stills, think on our behalf and console terrified humans by allowing them to take their 'selfies'. In short, they have started doing most, if not all, of the things that were used to distinguish humans as living, breathing beings. In fact, mobiles have an additional strength—they can communicate across long distances in nano-seconds. Since mobiles now preserve memory and humans shun it, the states that the humanistic-mobs of the last century created are busy erasing every trace of memory. Regimes in most countries have armies of mobile-set trolls responsible for doctoring people's memory. They have been cajoling people to forget history as it was and accept its myopic revisions. The mobile-wielders tell us that Gandhi brought about the division of India, that Godse was a great soul, that Nehru was an enemy of Indians, that ancient India had developed plastic surgery and high-flying planes, and many more enlightening things traditional history was unaware of. They also bombard on us accounts of how well things have been; and lest you doubt their portrayal of the ideologically sanitised progress, they produce, almost from nowhere, oven-fresh reports by international grading agencies on their wonderful achievements. Facts, fiction and fear make a unique cocktail. The current situation is that mobs will not remember, and if they do, mobiles will not allow them the luxury.

States that consciously encourage creating societies that forget to produce a critique of the system generate what ancient Latin described as hegemony. The term refers to the nature of power. In hegemonies, uncontested power becomes possible entirely out of the majority's self-approved willingness to promote the dominant ideas and perspectives. It is an insomniac social condition under which a vast majority is ready to impose the will of the rulers on the less powerful in the society. Hegemony that the amoral, complacent and unthinking majorities fuel results in a politico-psychological illness that ancient Greeks called 'hubris' among the ruling order. It looks like pride; but is much more than an ordinary person's pride in things good. It makes the ruling order forget why they are where they are. Hubris shuns dialogue. It avoids questions. It leads the ruling order to generate deafening self-righteous rhetoric and makes it entirely remorseless. Hegemonies headed by orders drunk on hubris start exhibiting these tendencies. Masses that were human even when they were mobs transform into lynch-mobs.

The incurable pride of the rulers combined with large sections of citizenry ready to crawl in order to fulfil their whims turn us into a mob-lynching society. The first victim of lynching is memory itself. It proposes new versions of history in which the ruling order must be depicted as 'the first', and anything that came before it as inconsequential and evil. If there are dissenters, they are placed under sharp assault by troll armies. If they continue to raise their voice, they are shown the gate as traitors. The Midas touch of a ruler heavy with hubris heightens the appetite for violence among the people he rules. When mobiles keep attacking the memory and minds of the masses every minute, the people become mobs, lynching everyone and everything that they suspect the ruler disapproves of.

Both hegemony and hubris have their peculiar histories. Since hegemony strives to ban all forms of critique, the suppressed questions pop up from strange quarters. They erupt naked from Una. They cry in agony from Unnao. They come in slogans from campuses and between the lines in press columns. But the ossified society that hegemony shapes is incapable of facing questions even as much as a pinch of salt at Dandi. Hubris was seen by the Greek society as a substance of tragedy. Its ending may generate fear, but little sympathy. The lynching mobs and the mobile-troll-armies forget that forceful erasure of memory eventually leads to the fall of hegemony and hubris. Silenced memory returns after every exile.

Crime Redefined

THE CORONAVIRUS, A PHENOMENON NOT FULLY UNDERSTOOD as yet, has forced humans to revisit many of their dearly held social habits and norms. It has also given rise to new norms, one of which relates to the notion of crime. In June 2020, Jeyaraj and Beniks, father and son, were allegedly beaten up, tortured and killed by Raghu Ganesh and Balakrishnan, police sub-inspectors posted at the Sathanukulam police station in Tuticorin. As was normal, the Tamil Nadu CID arrested the cops, the Madurai Bench of the Madras High Court ordered a probe and the CBI was asked to take over the case. What was not normal is the act that was perceived as the 'crime'. According to the business hour regulations in place to combat the virus, the victims had been late by half-an-hour in closing the shutters of their small shop, and the police officers felt duty-bound to point out the violation. A great tragedy for all the people involved—the victims, the murderers and their families—took place. The brutality involved can never be justified in a civilised society. That, however, cannot be said of the idea of crime in this instance. Decades ago, sociologist Emile Durkheim had pointed out that formal methods of dealing with crime may judge an act as a crime based on an 'airy nothing'. In *The Rules of Sociological Method*, Durkheim writes: 'Imagine a society of saints, a perfect cloister of exemplary individuals. Crimes, properly so-called, will there be unknown; but faults, which appear venial to the layman, will create there the same scandal that the ordinary offence does in ordinary consciousness. If, then, the society has the power to judge and punish, it will define these acts as criminal and will treat them as such'.* Had this been a one-off incident, the question would not have acquired such urgency. But there have been far too many incidents of mob-lynching, khaap-panchayat diktats denying individual freedom, fatwas by sectarian-orthodox bodies, and media trials and ostricisation of individuals holding different views, branding them 'anti-national'. This calls for deeper analysis. None of the aforementioned acts can be justified, but attempts to justify them could have been entertained had India not been a democracy and were it not accountable to constitutional norms. But the undeniable fact of history is that the immense diversity of people, culture, language and faith is held together as one nation by their allegiance to the Constitution that proclaims a non-negotiable guarantee to justice (social, economic and political), liberty (of thought, expression, belief, faith and worship) and equality (of status and opportunity). The preamble is 'absolute' in every sense of the term. What sadly is not in line with constitutional values is the tendentious interpretation of what crime is. I offer two apparently distinct but fundamentally linked cases.

---

* Emile Durkheim, *The Rules of Sociological Method*, translated by Sarah A. Solovay and John H. Mueller, edited by George E.C. Catlin (New York: The Free Press, 1938), p. 51.

The first of these deals with the term DNT, the other with UAPA. DNT stands for Denotified and Nomadic Tribes. It needs mention, particularly as we have crossed the 150th year of the mind-boggling misreading of the notion of crime by colonial administrators. In the 1820s, the East India Company administration felt threatened by the existence of stray groups of soldiers disbanded by the defeated Indian states who still possessed arms. In order to disarm them and to eliminate the potential challenge they would pose, the administration started a 'surveillance and survey project'. William Henry Sleeman (1788–1856), a soldier by training, was appointed to head the mission. Over the next few decades, Sleeman kept a meticulous record of armed clashes taking place in Central India and prepared a list of people, by their castes, involved in such incidents. In 1870, Lord Mayo, who had been sent to India as Viceroy, started working towards a legislation; and in October 1871, the first Criminal Tribes Act (CTA) was passed, comprising an annexure listing several communities and castes, drawing upon the lists previously made by Sleeman. The basic premise of the 1871 CTA was fundamentally flawed as it conceptualised crime as a hereditary occupation, that too based on Sleeman's deeply mistaken understanding of violent clashes and the myth of 'thugee' which he had successfully propagated among British readers through his books. The CTA went through multiple revisions till the last amendment to it in 1924; and in each of the amendments, the list of 'Notified castes/communities' continued to expand. The result was that all persons brought within its scope, irrespective of what they did or did not do, were seen by the law as 'criminal' or 'potentially criminal'. Strict area restrictions were imposed on them. Their long-distance movements were curbed. A larger section of them were detained in reformatory settlements (read soft prisons), and forced to contribute unpaid labour to various colonial projects like laying railway tracks, building dams and public buildings. Children and women were not exempted from this punishment, nor were they offered recourse to legal processes of redemption. The anger against this brutal treatment among the notified communities was so high that Lord Mayo was murdered by Sher Ali Afridi, held prisoner in Andaman, in February 1872, four months after the passage of the CTA. Afridi was hanged in March 1873. While Sleeman, Mayo and Afridi had all passed away by 1873, millions belonging to the Notified communities continued to languish in their settlements for decades, generation after generation. They were not freed immediately upon the proclamation of India's independence. That took some five years until, in August 1952, Jawaharlal Nehru decided to 'denotify' them and replace the CTA by a Habitual Offenders Act. Prior to the 1871 CTA, these communities had essentially been nomadic in their habits. Since 1952, they are referred to as the DNT— Denotified and Nomadic Tribes. The stigma attached to them persists. Their inclusion in either the ST or SC lists has been only partial. Without ownership of land and denied livelihood opportunities promised to them, they have kept surviving way below all indicators that define 'minimum human existence'. Their estimated population in India in 2020 was close to 14 crores. They are a testimony to the tremendous man-made disaster that mistaken notions of crime and criminality can cause.

The UAPA was passed with good intentions and was a mark of good international conduct. The United Nations, in response to the 9/11 (2001) attack by Al-Qaeda, sensing the need to have legislative backing for the anti-terrorism drive initiated by the member states, had requested the community of nations in November 2001 to form suitable laws. After several related UN resolutions in this regard, particularly the UN Security Council Resolution 1822 of 2008, India formed its UAPA. The amendment to it in 2019, passed through the Parliament in August, altered Section 35 of the UAPA to make it applicable to 'individuals' as well, as opposed to 'organisations' alone in the past. The results of this 'reinterpretation' are for us to judge. In April 2020, Masrat Zahra, a twenty-six-year-old photojournalist from J&K, was booked under its provisions. In Delhi, Meeran Haider and Safoora Zargar, young students from Jamia Milia Islamia, and Umar Khalid from JNU have been held using the UAPA. In Assam, Akhil Gogoi has been in prison since December 2019. Several prominent intellectuals have been booked using the provisions of the draconian law, claiming that they had incited violence during a meeting held in Pune in 2019. Among those booked are Gautam Navalakha and Anand Teltumbde. Hany Babu Musaliyarvittil Tharayil, a professor from Delhi University, was been picked up under the same provisions of the UAPA. AISA's Delhi president Kawalpreet Kaur too has been brought under the scanner. This is not a complete list of the individuals who have been arrested. The use of the UAPA against individuals who raise uncomfortable questions, coupled with a plaint judiciary, has now become a deadly instrument for suppressing thought and ideas.

During the NDA government of 2014–19, the killing of thinkers like Govind Pansare, M.M. Kalburgi and Gauri Lankesh had caused massive public protests. The arrests under UAPA do not, or rather cannot, create such protests, given the very nature of the law. Terrorist activities and sedition are terms that immediately place even a completely innocent individual under a heavy cloud of public suspicion, once charged so by the state. However, in the process, the state is branding free-thinking, holding divergent views, and dissent and disagreement on important public issues as crimes. As it happened in the past with communities that were perfectly innocent but were brought under the spectre of suspicion as 'being potentially criminal', the current regime is bringing dissent under labels like 'sedition' and 'terrorism'. Regimes, by the very nature of how they are constituted, will always find it convenient to use law with a semantic twist whenever possible. However, the Constitution and the fundamental rights guaranteed by it are bound to get seriously corroded in the process. Yet, to put it in correct historical sequence, governments are creatures of the Constitution. When a regime wilfully ignores the need to deepen it by respecting the guarantees given by it to the people who uphold the Constitution, it displays an imperfect understanding of the historical relationship between the people, the Constitution and their joint creature, the government. The blatant demonisation of dissent ultimately hurts those vying to hurt the foundation of democracy.

The Anti-CAA Protest

THE MOST RECENT INSTANCE OF PROTESTS AGAINST THE discriminatory and oppressive policies of the government in India was the protest against the Citizenship Amendment Act (CAA). Though the CAA was an abstract idea for common Indians in the beginning, the realisation that it would have a huge impact on the lives of millions of Indians soon moved them to action. I shall present here an overview of what it was all about and explain the nature of the discrimination implied in the CAA. Since I was one of the national conveners of 'We the People' which mobilised most of the peaceful protests, I would also like to state, with utmost humility, what the scope of the protest was.

The Citizenship Amendment Act has a history which goes back to the fag end of the colonial days. It was the Central Legislative Assembly of British India which first enacted the Foreigners Act in 1946, giving the central government the powers to deal with foreigners in India. Given the context of India's impending Partition, it was a confusing situation. The definition of the term 'foreigner' in the 1946 Act was rather enigmatic: 'one who is not Indian'. In December 1955, the Parliament of India enacted the Citizenship Act within the framework of Article 11 of the Constitution. The 1955 Act provided substantive and procedural norms for determination, acquisition and termination of Indian citizenship. Five decades later, in 2003, the central government promulgated the Citizenship Rules in order to provide better clarity regarding provisions related to the acquisition of citizenship. In 2015, building upon these provisions and rules, the Ministry of Home Affairs made amendments in the Passport Rules, 1950 and the Foreigners Order, 1948, allowing persons belonging to minority communities in Bangladesh and Pakistan entry into India. The entry was restricted to Hindus, Sikhs, Buddhists, Jains, Parsis and Christians, but not extended to Muslims and tribal communities seeking shelter in India. Additionally, the foreigners allowed entry into India were required to have faced religious persecution and should have entered India without valid documents on or before 31 December 2014. In July 2016, the Home Minister proposed an amendment in the Citizenship Act. The Citizenship (Amendment) Bill had been passed in the Lok Sabha, but had lapsed in May 2019, not having been cleared by the Rajya Sabha, the upper house of the Parliament.

The newly elected government placed the Bill once again before the Lok Sabha in December 2019, ironically just a day before International Human Rights Day (10 December). It was passed in the Lok Sabha with an overwhelming majority that the BJP had at its command, supported by 311 of 541 MPs. The Bill was also passed in the Rajya Sabha with 125 votes for and 105 votes against it. The next day, the President of India assented to the Citizenship (Amendment) Bill. Thus was born the Citizenship (Amendment) Act, 2019.

The amendments specifically pertain to Section 2 of the previously existing rules. The Act provides that the provisions of Foreigners Act, 1946 does not apply to persons belonging to minority communities—Hindus, Sikhs, Buddhists, Jains and Christian—from Afghanistan, Bangladesh and Pakistan. The CAA specified a cut-off date of 31 December 2014 for granting citizenship to such persons.

The compilation of the Assam Citizenship Register as part of the National Register of Citizens (NRC), as well as the process initiated by the Census of India for creating a National Population Register formed the backdrop for the CAA. Within weeks of the Modi 2.0 government's coming to power, the office of the Registrar of Census issued a notification under Rule 3 of the Citizenship Rules, 2003 for creating and updating the Population Register between 1 September and 30 September 2020. In the following month, the Government of Assam, along with the Union of India, updated the NRC for the residents of the state of Assam. This was done in compliance with a series of Supreme Court orders. In the Assam exercise, nearly 320 million individuals applied for inclusion in the citizenship register. The final list reportedly included only 311 million individuals, excluding 9 million. The information regarding the religion of individuals who were excluded and included in the citizenship register in Assam has not yet been made available.

On 20 November, the Home Minister of India announced plans for a pan Indian NRC. The announcement sent chills down the spine of individuals who care for a composite and secular society in India. The Home Minister tried to assure that the compilation of the NRC was being carried out merely to update the citizens list, and that no religion would be targeted. In less than three weeks, the Citizenship Amendment Bill was introduced in the Parliament and subsequently passed, making it the Citizenship (Amendment) Act. Phrases like 'chronology' and 'mark the timing' in the Home Minister's speech in the Parliament appeared to be a lazily concealed threat to the members of the Muslim community in India who did not possess formal documents to prove their citizenship.

The response to the Act from media, jurists, citizen groups and activists backed the arguments put forward by the opposition parties against the Act, apart from coming up with a few on their own. A bald summary of the issues and arguments raised in opposition to the CAA would be as follows:

One, the amendment violated the principles and basic values of the Constitution since it proposes to club together religion and citizenship.

Two, the criteria of classification to offer citizenship were not reasonable.

Three, there is no reason for including Afghanistan in the list of countries covered by the Act, and for leaving out other neighbouring countries such as Nepal, Bhutan, Myanmar and Sri Lanka.

Four, the Act lacks comprehensiveness, for it excludes several minorities, such as the tribal communities who face discrimination in Bangladesh, illegal migrants from Sri Lanka and several minorities within Islamic subgroups. The Act also makes no reference to ethnic groups such as Khasis, Garos, Brus, Chakmas, etc. who are all listed as minorities in the census of Bangladesh.

Five, the cut-off date stipulated by the Act has no logical basis.

Six, if religious persecution is the reason for granting citizenship, there is no reason to believe that the persecution would have come to an end after the cut-off date. The religion of any person is not enough ground to conclude that the persecution faced by them is religious; there are other nuances to persecution. Besides, in the case of those who migrated to India decades ago, it would be impossible to provide any proof of such persecution.

Seven, the people whose citizenship is to be determined by the CAA have been staying in Assam, West Bengal and elsewhere for a good three to four decades as of now.

Eight, the CAA would lead to a serious deterioration of India's relation with Bangladesh, and may put the lives of the non-Muslim communities covered by the Act in India's neighbouring countries at risk.

Finally, it was felt that the objective of CAA was discriminatory and unlawful. The classification created under the Act did not rationally align with the stated objective of the Act. Besides, it ignores persecution arising out of world views, culture, thought, expression and political turmoil in the subcontinent.

Criticism also emerged with reference to the vast range of India's undocumented people, such as the Adivasis, digitally marginalised nomadic communities, migrant labourers, the homeless, orphans and the zero-literacy section of the population. India has a huge emigrant population and it was made apparent when the lockdown was announced. All of them, it was argued, would be left out of the scope of the CAA. More importantly, the CAA brings religion into the definition of citizenship, specifically excluding Muslims and Jews, thereby creating space for legalising anti-Muslim bias in the proposed Citizen's Register and Population Register.

The more vocal critics argued that the recent series of legal actions of the BJP government, including the downgrading of the former Jammu & Kashmir state, and the Supreme Court verdict on the long vexed Babri Masjid–Ram Janmabhoomi dispute, clearly displayed the rapid unfolding of the Hindu project of the Rashtriya Swayamsevak Sangh (RSS). Similarly, the protracted clampdown on Kashmir as well as the Information Technology Act were seen as increased interference of the state in the personal domain of citizens. They pointed out the decline of the parliamentary system and the takeover of a more pronounced autocratic presidential system. The Information Technology Act states that the publisher or the one who transmits or causes to be published in the electronic form any material which is repugnant to government policies shall be punished, on first conviction, with imprisonment for a term which may extend to six months, or be fined up to two lakh rupees. In the event of a subsequent conviction, the imprisonment term may extend up to two years, and the fine up to five lakh rupees.

That the opposition to the CAA came from political parties, a section of the media, organised civil society groups and juries was not surprising. What surprised the establishment and the others outside was that students from many university campuses came out to protest, and that citizens who otherwise stay away from all political debates mobilised themselves to express their concerns about the CAA and the two registers (NRC and NPR) proposed by the government.

During the months when the CA Bill was on the anvil, the Muslim community in India remained on tenterhooks, deeply worried and anxious. The documents required for proving citizenship were not easy to collect. Many fake document 'factories' sprung up at the time. In those months, the Muslim community showed reluctance to come out in the open and discuss the CA Bill or question its necessity, while people of other faiths showed little interest in the issue. Of course, a major exception to this was Assam and the other north-eastern states which had closely witnessed the Citizens Register process unfold in the previous years. It was natural, therefore, that the very first non-party, non-organised reaction to the passing of the CAA came from Assam. In the first bout of protest in Guwahati, nearly seven lakh persons took to the streets. However, this was not adequately covered by the media. Soon, protests would erupt from several other states such as Kerala, Karnataka, Maharashtra, Gujarat, Madhya Pradesh and Jharkhand. Several State Legislative Assemblies joined in and passed resolutions or quasi resolutions rejecting the CAA, amounting to non-cooperation to the NRC and NPR. While the national electronic and print media, which had devoted themselves to towing the establishment's line, were not expected to deliver a faithful coverage of the protest, even they felt compelled to give considerable space to reports of the protest. Regional and local media presented a much more realistic picture. Social and digital media brought an even fuller reporting. Going by all the media reports, it was clear that the protest had been taking place in more than three hundred towns and cities across the country.

For months together, the protests showed no signs of receding, the protesters no signs of fatigue, as later in the case of the farmers' protest. The farmers protest went on for several months, with no signs of backing down. Considering that there was no single leader to the anti-CAA protests, and that there was no systematic coordination between one protesting group and another, it was quite mystifying as to how the movement that began on 12 December 2019 sustained itself over a period of several months. What was equally mystifying was how young Indians, who contributed significantly to BJP's electoral success in the Lok Sabha elections, stepped forward to counter the government's attempt to bury secularism as a basic principle of the Constitution. They made the protest their mission, kept formal political forces such as parties and unions out of the movement and led the movement from the front. The forms of protest invented by the young people were quite unique. A case in point is Shaheen Bagh. Equally remarkable was the use of social media, especially by those sections which did not previously use social media to articulate their political views. Shaheen Bagh in Delhi, where women sat in protest for weeks together with utmost moral courage, was also quite historic. Demonstrations replicating Shaheen Bagh sprang up in dozens of other cities and groups of citizens captured spaces on pavements, in parks, on open plots or wherever they could assemble. Young leaders and women protesters, who were a new phenomenon in India's political space, brought a new political idiom into circulation.

On the other hand, the government continued to be in denial, and was quite clueless about the extent of the discontent. It kept harping on its resolve to go ahead with the two registers, without formulating the rules necessary for the CAA to be implemented. The anti-CAA movement managed to prevent its implementation. In late 2020, the Home Minister stated that the government would start the process of compiling the Citizenship Register, and that the CAA would be brought in. It is difficult to decide if the BJP government was deliberately fanning the debate as a cover for its dismal economic performance.

It is another matter whether the judiciary would regain its courage to displease the regime and protect the spirit of the Constitution. There were nearly 130 public interest litigations challenging the CAA pending in the Supreme Court since December 2019. On the day the entire batch of petitions were admitted, the Supreme Court issued a notice to the Central

Government asking for a reply. The reply was produced, but the Supreme Court did not move any further beyond segregating the petitions.

Whether the new accent on federalism will eventually amount to a political alignment of small and big political parties uniting to counter BJP and its alienated allies is a matter that will interest TV anchors more than it appeals to the protesting groups. What was and is of utmost significance as India enters the third decade of the twenty-first century is the emergence of youth leadership at the forefront of an important national debate. It is equally significant that these young leaders are upholding humanism and constitutional values, and are articulating with unprecedented precision a non-sectarian and non-divisive politics. Such a fundamental political change has occurred before during the freedom struggle, inspired by Mahatma Gandhi, in the third decade of the twentieth century. Probably, a century later, in the third decade of the twenty-first century, another epistemic shift is set to emerge. The Indian political space has long been waiting for a complete change of political discourse. In the last four decades in particular, it has remained dominated by the idea of politics as the 'divide and rouse' game. The non-violent and spontaneous CAA protests that worked cohesively without allowing any overt coordination indicate that the political idiom in India is in for an epistemic change. Such is the impact of the protest, a mere two months of manifestation. It indicates that we are beginning to enter a new political era, one which is not proposed by the forces of Hindutva, but one that is heading towards greater humanism and empathy. Protests against discriminatory policies are not a new phenomenon in India. But, at this juncture, it is acquiring a heightened importance in defining the needs, urges and aspirations of a new India.

Citizenship Under Stress

In ancient Greek, *holos* meant 'entire' and *kaustos* meant 'burnt object'. The compound word formed out of the two was *holokauston*. Almost a millennium later, old French brought it in use as *holocauste*. However, the use of the word was limited to describing ancient liturgical practices. It was introduced in political discourse by Winston Churchill to describe the killing of people in Armenia during the First World War. The world understands it now as the elimination of nearly 1.7 million European Jews and Gypsies during Adolf Hitler's regime in Germany. In its initial phase, the project of mass extermination was introduced as the 'Final Solution'. Survivors of the Holocaust prefer the Hebrew word *shoah* (pronounced *sha-uh*) meaning 'a great calamity', preferring to avoid the theological connotation of any 'offering' implied by 'holocaust'. The Shoah, or the Sha-uh, was decidedly a shame for humanity and will be remembered for centuries as an inhuman act.

A question that has been bothering millions of Indians and a large number of others outside India is—Is India sliding towards some kind of *Sha-uh*? Is India destined to give up its cherished idea of secularism and deprive religious minorities of equal judicial relief and equal security of life and property? The very idea is so unnerving that one's tongue refuses to utter the words. Yet, the turn of events compels us to ponder the question.

The Citizenship (Amendment) Act, 2019 was passed by the Parliament with the help of the BJP's majority. It received the President's unquestioning assent and was also notified. The Supreme Court decided to respond to the 144 PILs with little sense of urgency. It offered four weeks' time for the government to respond. Even as the deadline passed, the response was awaited. The prime minister and home minister have repeatedly promised that no one in India would lose their citizenship due to the CAA. The CAA, they argue, is meant for those who have come from outside. But it is the religion-based acceptance of the persons from outside that the CAA formalises which is the source of worry. If this logic is extended to the exercise of the National Population Register and if the authority to declare any person a 'doubtful citizen' is given to the lower officials carrying out the NPR, the Sha-uh in India will have officially begun. Something similar happened when attacks were carried out by non-state warriors of Hindutva in Delhi and the police decided to play mere witness for nearly 72 hours. During those hours, arson and killing took place unchecked as so many people lost their lives. This, in Delhi, the capital of the country!

On 1 March 2020, Amit Shah declared that the CAA is final and no amount of protest and questioning can succeed in revoking it. Just a month earlier, he had stated in a TV interview that he would be willing to give an appointment within three days to anyone who wanted to discuss the CAA, NRC and NPR. Perhaps the government had woken up to the fact that the widespread protest was a genuine people's protest and not a manufactured political campaign supported by any party.

Two weeks after the protest began, many protesting groups felt that they should form a mutual support network. Thus, after discussions with Rajmohan Gandhi and Yogendra Yadav, we sent out a letter, and over a hundred organisations, groups and networks participated in a day-long meeting at the Press Club in Bombay on 29 December. A number of distinguished individuals with notable contributions to the Indian society were present there. We decided that all that will be done must be entirely peaceful, with no room for incitement of violence. We decided that the Indian flag and a copy of the Constitution be foregrounded in the protest. The name accepted for this network was 'We, the People of India/Hum Bharat ke Log'. Therefore, when the home minister stated that he would be willing to get into dialogue, we wrote to him: 'It appears from media reports that in your capacity as Home Minister of India, you have offered to allot time within three days to anyone who seeks time from your office, to discuss issues related to CAA. By this email, a small delegation of citizens, jurists and activists representing "We, the People of India" seeks an appointment with you at your earliest convenience'. We received the following reply from the director, Citizenship and Foreigners Division, Ministry of Home Affairs: 'You have made a request through e-mail to meet the Home Minister regarding the Citizenship (Amendment) Act, 2019. It is requested to kindly send a gist of the issues that you want to discuss in the proposed meeting.' We quickly sent a reply, giving a summary of our concerns: 'We would like to understand from the Hon. Home Minister: i) How does the CAA fit in with our Constitution? ii) How do the provisions of this Act match the stated objectives of the Act itself? iii) How does the Act fit in with the solemn promise made by the nation to the people of Assam in the Assam Accord of 1985? iv) How would this Act help persecuted minorities like Sri Lankan Tamils who seek refuge in India? v) What is the link between the proposed NPR and the NRC?' Further, we also requested the Minister i) To immediately put on hold the proposed operation of NPR ii) To assure the nation that the government does not plan to go ahead with the nation-wide NRC and iii) To repeal Section 14 of the Citizenship Act and all the changes brought in by CAA, 2019. We are still waiting for a follow-up regarding the promised meeting.

These concerns and demands have arisen from people in different states and districts over the last two months. Millions have taken out rallies, held meetings and sit-in protests; a large number of thinkers, intellectuals and mediapersons have written to the government voicing their concerns; several state assemblies have passed resolutions opposing the CAA, NRC and NPR; and various individuals and forums outside India have expressed their concerns. Yet, the government gives enough reason to believe that the RSS–BJP alliance's desire to change the fabric of the country from an inclusive one to one that discriminates people on the basis of religion will remain insatiate till the Constitution is rewritten. One hopes, and one can but hope as hope is endless, that the term 'Sha-uh' does not receive any currency in India.

Citizens' Register

Genocides often emerge out of ideas that seem noble when initially presented as just ideas. For instance, the complete desiccation of the indigenous population in the American continent was a result of Europe's idea of 'discovering new worlds and civilising them'. They emerge when a large mass of people surrenders their sense of justice to the spellbinding charm of a leader. The Holocaust brought about by the Nazi rule in Germany was one such. Genocides also emerge out of people's sense of loyalty to a bunch of difficult-to-define ideas such as 'nation', 'religion' or 'progress'. The gruesome history of mass punishment meted out to several nomadic castes and communities during the colonial era belongs to this genre. In all these instances, the frontrunners of violence are not necessarily some wicked characters or murderous criminals. In most cases, they are perfectly normal humans diligently engaged in their assigned duty. What make their individual acts of normal duty amount to ghastly collective violence are not the ideas they think they are serving—science, nation, religion, progress—but the hatred guiding their acts. Even good ideas, if driven by hatred, invariably result in crime against humanity. The National Register of Citizens in India has started treading that path now.

The roots of NRC go back to the time when India attained independence. The Census of India prepared a National Register of Citizens in 1951 as part of the first census exercise after the Partition of India. At the time, it was an excellent idea as it helped prepare a preliminary voters' list for the country. To have the State Register of Citizens made for Assam subsumed in the NRC also seemed a decent idea. But it comes with the caveat that one must have been a resident in Assam prior to March 1971 or be able to establish blood kinship with such a person. But half a century later, the implications of that idea have changed radically, even if the updating of the NRC is placed under the monitoring of the Supreme Court. The year 2019 is not 1951. Both India and the world have profoundly changed over the last seven decades. One of the major changes has been the phenomenon of international migration. World Migration Report (2018) produced with the data available from UN agencies opens with the sentence: 'International migration is a complex phenomenon that touches on a multiplicity of economic, social and security aspects affecting our daily lives in an increasingly interconnected world'. It goes on to state that nearly 244 million persons now live outside the country of their birth. In 1971 (the cut-off year for Assam), this number was only a third of what it is at present.

The data in the report, based on the official figures provided by the State parties to the UN, show that the highest number of international migrants are based out of India (16 million), followed by Mexico (12.5 million), Russian Federation (10.5 million), China (9.5 million), Bangladesh (7 million) and Pakistan (5.5 million). These figures include legal as well as detected illegal migrants. If these figures are reliable, the claims by various political parties in India that the number of illegal immigrants from Bangladesh now resident in Assam and West Bengal is close to 5 million or more—out of the total of 7 million Bangladeshi migrants all over the world—is absolutely preposterous. Such exaggerated claims must be dismissed at once. The exercise of 'scrutiny' revealed 1.9 million cases of 'not-registered' individuals in Assam; this number is expected to come down dramatically after more rounds of scrutiny. This yawning gap between the mischievous claims and verified data is strikingly similar to the case of 'black money'—where pre-demonetisation claims suggested enormous amounts, but post-demonetisation data proved otherwise. The exercise served merely to dig the grave for small and informal businesses while not tracing any black money. Similarly, the NRC verification exercise may eventually destroy the citizen's faith in the state, and not reduce illegal migration at all.

The conceptual frameworks that the terms 'nation' and 'nationalism' had in 1951 were heavily influenced by the contemporary history of freedom struggles in various Asian and African countries. Over the last seven decades, those ideas have changed too. 'Opening up' and not 'closing down' is now at the heart of national economies and, to that extent, national polities too. International movement of capital, knowledge, technology and workforce is now seen as a positive feature in an economy. International migration has become an essential and irreversible factor in the growth and economic security of every nation. India's economy too has benefitted enormously by contributions from the Indian diaspora. Given this new economic reality, to put millions of hardworking residents of a region through a humiliating scrutiny for verifying their citizenship is an exercise in futility. The fact that it is detrimental for the economy of the north-eastern and eastern states—the states that have already lagged behind in economic growth—has been tragically overshadowed by the BJP's euphoria in its recent electoral success in those states.

The NRC exercise is flawed also because it is based on a very narrow understanding of the livelihood practices and cultural history of the region. During the colonial era, the administration compelled nomadic populations in central and north-western India to acquire sedentary habits by imposing 'zoning' and other restrictions on their movement. As a result, the communities that had once been integral to the supply chain of the Indian economy came to be labelled as 'criminal tribes'. We cannot overlook the fact that long-distance migrations, particularly in the region that is famous for the frequent flooding of the Brahmaputra, have been a common phenomenon throughout the known history of our civilisation. The influence of Buddhism is a testimony to the incessant mobility of people in the region. While the region, the ecology and the people have not changed much over the years, they are now distributed across the countries of India, Bangladesh and Myanmar. In order to improve the economic profile of Assam and other north-eastern states, it is necessary for the rest of India to understand that permeable borders are intimately tied to the livelihood practices of the communities in Assam and surrounding areas. Therefore, the NRC exercise could have benefitted from greater empathy from the state.

However, the current dispensation in the Ministry of Home Affairs has a different view of things. It is driven by a passion to prove that Hindus from Bangladesh migrated to India due to religious persecution, while the Muslims did so without much reason, eventually settling in 'our' country as 'illegal' migrants. The emotionally charged language—'chun-chun ke marenge' and 'ghar mein ghus kar marenge'—coming from the Prime Minister has fuelled the imagination of the Ministry of Home Affairs. As a result, what would have otherwise been an inane census exercise has now turned into a political slugfest and a contest of patriotic one-upmanship. In the process, India is being pushed into a situation that will render thousands of families desperate. The amount of hatred generated in the process among religious communities will keep the region a live tinderbox ready to erupt into flames year after year. Besides, the process will also drive a nail deep into India's already fractured relations with our eastern neighbours. The economic and diplomatic losses we face, along with human rights violations affecting thousands of families, must be weighed against the negligible gains that the NRC process is likely to produce, if India is to stake claim to being a great nation.

'Fear Not'

Delhi *is* charming. Its charm has not failed to fascinate a single soul. The Pandavas who are believed to have ordered the building of the shining Indraprastha city somewhere close to the present-day Purana Qila, Qutb ud-Din Aibak who got the tall brick-minar constructed, the Lodis who created the Shisha Gumbad in the exquisite parks, the Mughals who gave Delhi the Lal Qila among many majestic structures and the British who left behind Edwin Lutyens's Delhi for us, had all come under Delhi's charm and, in turn, added their bit to it. For over a thousand years, and probably much longer in its uncertain past, Delhi has fascinated the rest of India. It will not be an exaggeration to say that all roads in India lead to Delhi, the place, the history and the legend. Delhi, despite its polluted air, its political skullduggery, its many masks and its history of massacres and riots, continues to enchant India.

My first visit to Delhi was over half a century ago. In January 1968, as a young college student, I went there to meet Lalita Gouri Shastri. It was two years after Lal Bahadur Shastri had met with an untimely death. In her reception of me—a strange lad from the south with awkward Hindi, terrified of the large city—she was warm, affectionate and as simple as a rustic song. As I was leaving her, she gently touched my head to bless me and said, 'daro mat', fear not. In the limited time I had before I had to catch my return train, I went around looking at as many monuments as a quick rickshaw ride allowed. Most of them created a sense of awe in my mind. I could not reconcile the contrast between Lalita-ji's touching simplicity and the awe-striking monuments of Delhi.

Is Delhi the legacy of Nadir Shah's ferocity or the melancholic love of Mirza Ghalib? I have often wondered if Ghalib was not speaking to the Shahs of the past when he wrote in his lonely last years: *'terey vade pe jiye hum, to yeh jano, zhuta jana/ke khushise mar na jate etabar hota'* (It was your promises that kept me alive, though I knew they were pure lies. Had they been true, would I not have died of delight)? In Delhi, one does not have to be a poet of Ghalib's genius to catch a lie. Every Lalita Devi in Delhi has the courage to face the terror of every Shah; every Ghalib has the wits to know the lies pandered as promises. The two together give Delhi its unique strength. Others have added but monuments to the city saddled with history. It appears that today, this unique strength is returning to Delhi in full measure. It runs in equal degree among the courageous university students in protest and the steadfast women of Shaheen Bagh, full of fortitude. Through their courage, action, speech and idealism, they are saying to the millions of Indians 'daro mat'—a message as simple as it is great. Shaheen Bagh is no monument, no exquisite public place created to charm the world. It is a locality, barely familiar even to the residents of Delhi until recently, and not unlike thousands of other neighbourhoods across the length and breadth of India that come alive through their everyday ordinariness. And, indeed, the whole of India has suddenly woken up to the realisation that there is a Shaheen Bagh in every nook and corner of this country.

I was in Bombay a few days back, and saw several thousand women following the Shaheen Bagh form of protest there. The following day, I was in Sangli in south Maharashtra, where I met hundreds of women who had turned a pavement outside the old railway station into their own Shaheen Bagh. That evening, when I returned to Dharwad in North Karnataka, I was told that nearly two thousand women have undertaken a Shaheen Bagh satyagraha. It seemed as if Shaheen Bagh is being invited into every town in India. It is as if every Indian town is telling its neighbour, 'daro mat'. This is precisely what puts an end to the awe and fear instilled by the Shahs of history; and once the fear is gone, the lies become easy to call out.

The CAA, the proposed NRC and the NPR were opposed in the Parliament by several political parties. Once the CA Bill became an Act—the CAA—it received, as expected, criticism from jurists, journalists and several civil society formations. All of that was not new to the set grammar of Indian politics. But when girl students on university campuses and the otherwise ordinary and apolitical people started opposing it vehemently, one realised that there was something unique about this protest. When the Supreme Court treated the 144 petitions related to the CAA as just any matter, there was neither much dismay nor much surprise. But when the satyagraha inspired by Shaheen Bagh started surfacing from every small and big town in the country, one knew that a new language of political expression had emerged. When state after state of the Indian federation expressed its disapproval of NRC and NPR, it felt like familiar actors playing out an unfamiliar scene. But when a totally uncoordinated, leaderless bunch of people started mobilising themselves, holding the tricolour in one hand and a copy of the Constitution in the other, in different corners of the country, one found a compelling reason to believe that people are openly challenging the authorities, a first since the time of Mahatma Gandhi. Unmistakably, the great phenomenon inscribed in the Constitution as 'We, the people ...' is back with us. It is chanting tunes of courage and compassion; it is shouting an emphatic 'no' to the 'divide and rouse' politics. Shaheen Bagh is a metaphor for an epistemic change in the Indian political discourse. For India, a fundamental change is unfolding before our eyes. Thank you, courage. Thank you, Shaheen Bagh.

Thinking Citizens

It is difficult to say whether orthodoxy, and its nemesis dynamism, is more characteristic of a society than the ideas it receives and internalises. We believe that any major shift in a society's material conditions will necessarily bring about a shift in all the ideas that constitute its foundations. But history has witnessed instances where social progression was not accompanied by a corresponding shift in foundational ideas. Post-War Europe is a classic example of this mismatch. History also has examples where ideas have moved ahead while societies lagged miserably behind. Different varieties of colonial modernity offer a wide spectrum of testimony to such mismatch. Since social formations as well as the architecture of ideas are shaped by humans, both kinds of mismatch result in tragic consequences for a large number of people. In our immediate context, citizenship is a case in point.

A quick view of its evolution tells us that *'citisein'*, the old French origin of the term, was used to mean 'the inhabitants of a city or a town'. This in turn was based on the idea of home as a mental image of close relations. *'Domus'* was the Latin term for home and *domicillium* for dwelling. This was later picked up by the legal language in European countries and the idea of home as 'residence from which one has no intention to shift' gained stability. Well until what British history describes as a 'hundred years of war', the idea of citizen and the idea of habitat held mutual correspondence. But the war had created the need for a steady number of soldieries, and the number of soldiers under royal command entirely depended on the stability of revenue. This fiscal need led England and France to move from taxation on farm yield to taxation on farm land. Yields can vary; but the area of land under cultivation would be relatively steady. With the changed tax laws, the meaning of 'citizen' moved closer to ownership of land and tax-paying ability. This was good practice for Europe during the seventeenth and eighteenth centuries. But the same cannot be said of its implications for colonial India during the nineteenth century.

The British colonial administrators in India noticed that a large part of the population was nomadic in nature. In addition to the large-scale religious pilgrimages of sects, communities were seldom rooted to a single specific habitat. The colonial administration felt that if these communities do not have a predictable land relationship, bringing them under the tax regime would be difficult. Once this realisation hit them, the regime did everything to bring them under control and change their nomadic habits so that they became sedentary in thought and act. In the background of the wars, cessations of states, building roads and rail tracks, pressing English in law and education, the colonial administrators kept themselves busy isolating all non-sedentary communities. An officer named William Henry Sleeman was specially appointed to keep watch on these 'thugs'. Given his position of authority and his unmatched enthusiasm in hunting for anything nomadic, it was no surprise that the *thugee* myth took roots in a few decades. The legitimacy acquired by the stereotypes he had floated was evident in the Criminal Tribes Act of 1871. It had a sizeable list of communities designated 'criminal'. It included the transgender 'Hizras', coin-making 'Meenas', stone mason 'Wodders' and horse-mounted traders 'Sansis'. Other communities were brought under the draconian provisions in subsequent versions of the Criminal Tribes Act (CTA). A total of 190 communities were subjected to the provisions, kept in reformatory prisoner colonies—appropriately called 'settlements'—branded as criminals and used for unpaid labour on public civil works. Even after the country gained independence, the communities wrongly branded as criminals continued to languish in their settlements with meagre access to civil rights. A large mass of our own working population had thus been turned into lesser citizens. In 1952, they were 'denotified', the CTA was slightly amended and replaced by a Habitual Offenders Act, carrying the same spirit as its predecessor.

The point I am trying to make here is not that nothing much has been done for the Denotified Nomadic Tribes. While, that indeed is the case, I am trying to focus on the continued process of restricting the meaning of the term 'citizen'. The Indian Constitution, in its most idealistic sweep of vision, proposes for all of us full citizenship status. However, in the working of laws and regulations, it has routinely been getting truncated. A look at the plight of communities that do not speak any of the scheduled languages as their mother tongue will prove this point. The state is uninterested in creating access to education in their own languages for them. So, their linguistic citizenship is compromised. Our courts do not have law interpreters for everyone. Those who fail to understand the intricacies of law courts automatically become legal non-citizens. Those who have bank accounts and Aadhaar cards have at least a partial economic citizen status. Those who do not have them lose out on this account.

Orson Welles's 1941 American film *Citizen Cane* is a haunting portrayal of isolation, centring on the idea of citizenship within a society, where capital and media wield true power. The neoliberal economies have been fast turning very large sections of the society into lesser citizens. Of course, this is a global and, to a large degree, an irreversible phenomenon. This has real-life implications on people, and are not just digital numbers printed in grey ink by a chip-driven printer. The process of excluding citizens, aided by technologies that turn them into mobs, has become even more ruthless due to nationalistic jingoism and theocratic bigotry which are quickly getting normalised. Coercive tax regimes further enable the repetition of such history.

In an ideal world, democracies are expected to enlarge and broaden the citizenship rights for every segment of the society. This is a marvellous idea; but our world has precariously veered away from the ideal. So much so, that thinking different thoughts, saying different prayers, eating different food, dressing differently, and remembering different heroes and histories are seen by the minions of the state as sedition or treason. The State itself is asking for greater snooping rights, whether it is in Turkey, Egypt, Russia, US or in our own country. There was a time when those who were targeted by the State had some constitutional guarantees to help them. But while the society has changed, the idea of constitutional democracy has not kept pace with it.

A century and a half ago, Karl Marx used the term 'the have-nots' to describe social segments deprived of all citizenship rights. Ambedkar, on his part, used the term 'dalit'. How does one describe, in our present context, all the different classes of people being treated as second-class citizens? We can probably call them, for linguistic ease, *gastflects*—the ones afflicted by GST, the prized trophy of the current dispensation. These include the ones who have no jobs or housing, no access to education and healthcare, no Aadhaar card, no legal remedy, no possibility of restructuring their farm loans and no real say in forming governments. Add to these, the victims of widespread intolerance and minority-baiting. Hubris and hegemony are in the air and innocent citizens are facing increased discrimination. History is a habitual offender; yet it is the oppressed people in different eras who cause the change of its course.

Migration and the Post-Democracy State

THE PRE-HISTORIC *HOMO SAPIENS* SPREAD OUT FROM THEIR place of origin to different continents braving unimaginable odds, becoming the avante garde in the process of evolution of life. Had they not risked their lives and spread out, we would not have been what we are today. Their original migration, and all the subsequent migrations stretched over thousands of years, have been at the heart of the human advent. It was but natural that at the dawn of history known to us, the memories of those long migrations and what humans had learnt out of them formed the universe of knowledge. Whether it is the Ramayana for India or the Odyssey for the Greeks, epics normally mark the inauguration of great civilisations. As their generic hallmark, epics present heroic stories of great migrations. Throughout known history, migrations have spurred, aided and advanced ideas, knowledge-stock, culture and the horizons of human thought.

During the relatively recent history of the last five hundred years, the phenomenon of migration has brought people and nations to the threshold of modernity. In post-industrial societies, outward migration has significantly affected economic transitions as well as political trends. Colonialism transformed the way traditional communities in several continents perceived themselves and aspired to organise themselves as political entities. Large-scale migrations from Europe to Australia and North America also contributed to these historic developments. Almost as a counterforce to colonial history, migrations from Africa, Asia and Eastern Europe to the Western world reached an unprecedented scale in the twentieth century.

The United Nations compiles a report on migration every two years. The report for 2017 recorded that approximately 258 million persons now live outside their country of birth. Nearly three quarters of all international migrants are of working age. The high-income countries hosted 64 per cent, or nearly 165 million, of the total number of international migrants worldwide. It should be of interest to us that Indians top the international migration chart, with 16 million Indians living outside India, described as diaspora. India is followed by Mexico (12 million), the Russian Federation (11 million), China (10 million), Bangladesh (8 million), and Pakistan and Ukraine (6 million each). In India, the aspiration to migrate out of India for education and employment opportunities is often seen as a positive trait. However, the UN report confines itself to international migration alone. Within India, if we were to take into consideration inter-state and inter-lingual migrations, the magnitude would be much higher. Taken together, more than half of the Indian population today are probably migrants. Historically, migration has quickened the human advent and contributed to global cultural diversity. However, since implicit in it is a challenge to the idea of nation, the nation-state does not take kindly to migrant populations.

In August 2019, the Donald Trump administration in the USA introduced a regulation that allowed authorities to indefinitely detain migrant families who illegally cross the border. The regulation replaced an older court agreement known as the Flores Settlement which limited the duration for which migrant children could be detained. The new regulation sends out a chilling message to families attempting to migrate to USA from the rest of the world. Trump's statement regarding this regulation would be hard to comprehend even for an American: 'One of the things that will happen, when they realise the borders are closing—the wall is being built, we are building tremendous numbers of miles of wall right now in different locations—it all comes together like a beautiful puzzle.' Clearly, the post-democracy State has commenced a war on migration.

The seeds of this war on migration were sown by colonial capitalism. In India, colonial rule brought in ideas of citizenship which adversely affected the lives of traditionally nomadic communities and ended up stigmatising them. Moreover, the colonial idea of education and urban settlements as driving engines of productivity influenced agrarian population to migrate towards urban spaces. Thus, during the process of colonialism, three distinct varieties of migration emerged as inherent social features of modern nations. During the post-colonial times, these categories acquired greater complexity as hitherto unknown patterns of migration started emerging. These include forced displacement of peripheral communities affected by development projects, migration resulting out of heavy resource-exploitation activities such as mining, migration resulting from endangerment of traditional livelihood practices such as agriculture and sea-farming, migration related to rising economic aspirations and related education needs and, finally, migration induced by the desire to escape caste oppression. In other words, migration is both a factor contributing to economic and educational betterment as well as an indicator of deprivation and marginalisation of communities.

The phenomenon of migration occupies a central place not just in India but in countries all over the world. But the post-democracy state is in no mood to extend sympathy to inward migration. When no nation is willing to favour inward migration, people of all nations will be deprived of fair opportunities to migrate outward. Such a static demographic condition, apart from visibly harming economies, will invisibly hurt the principle of diversity necessary for evolution. The worst victims will be women and children. At present, nearly half—48.4 per cent—of international migrants are women. Female migrants outnumber males in all regions except Africa and Asia. It is an easy guess that when the number of women migrants goes up, the number of migrant children too will rise proportionately. However, if the Trumps and the Shahs of the world insist on building walls on international borders, creating detention camps and piling up regulations hostile to migrants, the post-democratic nations will inevitably reverse the advent of man.

Philosophers and historians have argued in recent decades that humans have come to the end of history. A couple of years ago, members of the scientific community got together and announced the definitive commencement of the Anthropocene, a euphemism for the end of life and the natural diversity of species. The post-democratic state is, unfortunately, hastening this end by building visible and invisible walls between people and between nations. The term 'nation' appears to have travelled an unholy distance from its original meaning 'people'. Now, the nations that are getting increasingly suspicious of people are precisely the ones whose governments brandish 'nationalism'. The 'beautiful puzzle', wrapped in the scornful chuckles of Trump, is beginning to manifest itself as our charred future.

The Present and the Past

THE YEAR 2020 IS, NO DOUBT, THE YEAR OF THE Coronavirus, with its intent of annihilating the human species. It is also the year when scientists formally announced the decisive commencement of the Anthropocene, the annihilation of Nature by human beings. In the complex plot of these two terminal wars, there are other sub-plots. These include the war between the ultra-right and the democrats in many countries; the war over the idea of citizens as settled individuals as opposed to a definition inclusive of nomads and migrants; and the war between theocratic and secular ideas of state. Even more sub-plots revolve around gender, class, identity, language and history. It would be a great challenge for any future historian to provide a full depiction of 2020— such is the enormity and the magnitude of events happening all around us. Since the present moment is so overburdened by the history it is generating, it is unlikely that it takes a moment to recall the past. Memory 'recollected' often tends to disrupt the plot of narratives being constructed in the present, and memory 'brushed aside' can call into question the authenticity of such narratives.

The world may not find time to recall that it is more than seventy-five years since the Allies had a conclusive win in the Second World War, and on 30 April 1945, Adolf Hitler ended his life. We are too busy to remember that when Peter Coombs liberated the inmates of the Bergen–Belsen concentration camp, he found that the Jews and other prisoners inside had been struck by a great typhoid epidemic. He reported that every day at least three hundred people had died in the camp, and found more than ten thousand corpses lying inside. The soldiers who buried the bodies did not even have gloves as protective gear. On the same day, seventy-five years later, India's three-week lockdown reached a technical halt.

Worth remembering too are a couple of literary works, not because they may otherwise be forgotten but more because we may remain unaware of our own circumstances. One of them was by the French novelist and thinker Albert Camus. Published in Paris by Gallimard publishers as *La Peste* in 1947, and in Stuart Gilbert's English translation as *The Plague* in 1948, the slim novel took the world by storm. Camus, its young writer, had been working on it since he was twenty-nine and had plans of writing a novel in order to 'redeem the plague'. The readers of his time and later immediately recognised that the plague Camus wrote about was that of fascism, though he outwardly referred to the long history of epidemics afflicting his own Algeria. A less spectacular manifestation of its success was the Nobel Prize awarded to the forty-four-year-old Albert Camus, while a more striking one was that several generations of young persons in the world, trapped in their own existential crises, invariably turned to the protagonist of *The Plague*, Dr Bernard Rieux, in the city of Oran, and his words — 'It is up to me to do what I can'. Do not escape, please, just continue to fight, Camus said to his readers as the stench of Bergen–Belsen would have overwhelmed Europe seventy-five years ago.

The other book that harkens me is Eric Blair's political parable. He was, though by a miniscule degree, our own Bihari Babu. Born in Motihari, Bihar, to an English father and French-Burmese mother, Blair was moved to England for his education. Having somehow finished his schooling, at nineteen, he chose to join the Indian Imperial Police Service and sought posting in Burma. He would have probably continued in the IIPS had it not been for his failing health, which made him leave British India and settle for a career as a journalist and writer using the pseudonym George Orwell. It stuck forever to him as well as in the world's literary history. Orwell's *Animal Farm* was published in 1945. The French translation of the book appeared in 1947, the same year as Camus's *The Plague* did. If Camus's subject was fascism in Western Europe, Orwell's was the totalitarian communism in the USSR. He deliberately chose the subtitle *Union des républiques socialistes animales*, which when abbreviated as URSA is the Latin word for 'bear', the cultural symbol of Russia. In fact, he wrote to Arthur Koestler—who shared with Orwell an utter dislike for attacks on decency and human dignity in any coercive state—that the publication of the French translation was being delayed due to 'political reasons'. George Orwell was born in 1903 and lived till 1950. Albert Camus was born ten years later, in 1913, and lived for exactly a decade after Orwell was gone. A temporal coincidence, nothing more! However, it is no coincidence that between the two of them, they offered a complete method of fighting fascism and totalitarian regimes. Camus provided the world the philosophical basis for resistance, quite dramatically depicted in his *The Myth of Sisyphus* (1942). Orwell provided us the vocabulary to rip apart totalising regimes: 'Big Brother', 'thought police', 'thought crime', 'the Ministry of Happiness', 'memory hole', 'double-think' and 'newspeak' are all his coinages, that now boast a unique place in the English language.

In the spring of 2020, as the world was experiencing the pandemic, seventy-five years since the world saw its most brilliant political forensic analysts, the shadow of democratically sanctioned dictatorships looming over every other country, we found it hard to recall that just three-quarters of a century ago, the world had seen it all. In 2020, as we groaned under the epidemic of thought viruses and the violence erupting out of the large-scale contamination it has caused, we forgot Orwell and Camus who faced the same, if not more brutal, situation in their time and yet enriched human thought through their courage in wielding the pen.

Another remarkable writer of their generation was the American Hemingway. His *The Old Man and the Sea* (1950) appeared in English just a few years after *Animal Farm* and *The Plague*. Ernest Hemingway received the Nobel Prize for Literature just a couple of years before Camus did. In 2020, as we struggled, under the unfathomable economic misery and the attack of a natural virus unprecedented in history, as we saw a world where national boundaries are sealed like prisons, as we learnt to look at every 'other' as contaminated and a potential threat, what we needed to recall was that between 30 April 1945, when Hitler ended his life, and 1950, the likes of Orwell, Camus and Hemingway had given the world a new sensibility, a new way of coping with the many plagues of their time and boundless hope. When determined, an old man can. If determined, an old civilisation can, too, no matter how deadly the virus!

A March to the Future or a Leap Backward?

It is not just as chronological coincidence that Ivan Illich's *Deschooling Society* (1970) and Michel Foucault's *Discipline and Punish* (1975) appeared within a few years of each other. One was an attack on the idea of school as a delivery system for knowledge, while the other an attack on prison as a delivery system of a society's well being. Both proved extremely influential in turning intellectual attention towards concepts and institutions that are considered bedrocks of civilised society. It needs no mention that neither of these works was against the principles—of social well-being, in Foucault's case, and knowledge, in Illich's case—but the institutional travesty of those principles. In questioning the institutional manifestations of those ideas, they were questioning the concepts that constitute modernity, thereby showing the underbelly of the conceptual complex on which various visions and ideas of the modern world are based. The politics of these interrogations pointed to how the diabolic sits together with the sanguine in what we think is normal in the modern world, and how the state has constantly overreached its initial brief as delineated by the people who sanctioned the creation of nation-states from nations. One of the many instruments used by the state to encroach on its people is the census. Carried out by the state, apparently as an ideology-free statistical exercise with no more than functional significance, rarely it is what it looks like.

If etymology is any help in analysing a concept, we have for census its close etymological link with the term 'censor'. The Latin root *'censere'*, meaning 'to assess, to value, to judge', gradually became *'censor'*, meaning 'to assess, to take a measure of someone' as long back as the fifth century CE. Its presence in Middle French and Old English gave it an additional meaning of 'moral judge'. The official appointed for passing moral judgements was called 'censor' during the seventeenth century, a time when one's church affiliation became a crucial factor in determining one's social status in France as well as England. The incessant wars between the Catholic France and the Protestant England increased the bureaucratic importance of the censor. By the nineteenth century, in the political context of Europe after Napoleon, the term split into two—one meaning 'state official in charge of scrutiny and suppression of citizens', and the other meaning 'a count of citizens and their assets'; one becoming 'censor' as we recognise it in the 'censor board' and the other 'census' as we understand since the second half of the nineteenth century.

When the Census of India was first carried out in the 1860s, the intention of the colonial rulers was not just to know how many persons lived in the subcontinent under their control. It was also to understand how the population is divided into different sub-groups, religions, castes and conventions.

The 1860s was a complex decade, both for India and the government that had assumed authority over it. In Europe, the Franco-Prussian war had changed political equations, with England gaining greater significance within the 'community of nations', and 'nationalism' acquiring greater legitimacy. In India, the colonial power was in search of land to lay rail tracks and build industrial forests, listing all those communities that came in the way. Previously, in the 1830s and 1840s, William Henry Sleeman had compiled a list of dangerous communities by devoting himself to recording every scuffle, every clash that involved the use of weapons. The myth of 'thugee' was made immensely popular by Sleeman's books published in England. His list was used by Lord Mayo in enacting the first Criminal Tribes Act in October 1871. Mayo was murdered a few months later, in 1872. But he left behind a lasting instrument for use by rulers in India—the Census of India. Carried out first in 1872, the decadal census acquired an unparalleled status as an instrument for deciding state policy.

The first comprehensive census was conducted in 1881. The features enumerated kept shifting—from dangerous animals to number of villages, from death tolls in epidemics to the number of religious establishments. Counting, irrespective of what was counted, acquired official sanction and the data thus collected acquired a truth value, despite major gaps, erroneous computations and flawed methodology. The exercise of census for a country like India was never easy. It was even less during the pre-Independence period when literacy levels were extremely low and the mutual trust between the subjects and the rulers even lower. After Independence, the task was given to the Ministry of Home Affairs, the Registrar General and the Census Commissioner. Thus came into being the Census of India Act of 1948, a testimony to the significance of the census exercise as a necessary aid for governance. The most important census from the perspective of demographic data held during the colonial rule was the 1931 Census, which had gathered invaluable information on castes and communities. The credit for the conceptualisation of sociological enumeration goes partly to the capacity developed by the Census office, and partly to the development of anthropology as a discipline, which, by the 1920s, had acquired an outstanding status due to new breakthroughs made by European scholars in the subject.

Census acquired much more importance after India became independent, as its economic model had made five-year plans as its cornerstone. For providing rationale to these plans, data coming out of the decadal counts was found to be useful. Besides, despite the gaps and deficiency in the census methods, decade-by-decade comparison of data indeed came in handy to develop a perspective on issues like population, literacy, agriculture, animal husbandry, irrigation and language. One has reason to thank the census data for enabling discussions and debates on the economy, development and social transformation. In a country that had become a nation by bringing together in its fold several hundred states, and which had one of the largest populations at the time, such an 'objective' reference-data was most essential. Keeping with the development of other institutions that aimed to promote a democratic ethos within the country, the norms, regulations, procedures and outcomes of the census were developed to make it an exercise to empower the people. For instance, the data related to literacy levels in various states helped in setting achievable goals, which contributed, over time, to their improvement. Census data proved to be a reliable means through which policies could be formulated regarding reservations and poverty reduction schemes.

A March to the Future or a Leap Backward? 67

More importantly, various activist groups and organisations, trade unions, farmers cooperatives and media critical of the government too depended heavily on census data for building their campaigns, activities and arguments. Thus, for several decades, the census played a major role in strengthening welfare and democracy in India.

However, the census in India always had the challenge of scale. The large population spread over a large geographical area invariably made the exercise a nightmare for the Commissioner of Census. It had to depend on a large number of school teachers as enumerators. Hailing as they did from diverse language backgrounds, it was a challenge to turn them into 'trained enumerators' within a few months. Besides, over the past decades, every census had introduced new features, bringing in a new set of questions on age, religion, income, household assets, marital status, gender distribution and so on. Each of these areas deserved a census in itself. So, every decennial census was, in fact, a mix of several enumerations carried out at the same time and analysed to produce 'finished data' in record time. The volume of the data produced, their analysis, preparation for the next census and discussions to remove ambiguities in questionnaire required time; and the nine-year gap between two census exercises felt too short with every passing census. This pushed individual ministries such as the ministries for rural development, health, cottage industries and education to develop their own methods for specific-purpose enumeration through panchayats and taluka-level government offices. By the 1980s, similar work was also being taken up by various commissions to gather more authentic data, such that the government's dependence on the Registrar General's office decreased significantly. Data thus collected came in handy for specific situations—

for instance, to define poverty and to adjust poverty lines. Besides, the expansion of government functions and the growing network of government-created institutions, which produced greater data inputs in a short time, made the census seem inadequate as a means of gathering the necessary statistical information. Perhaps, the best use of the census data was made, since the 1980s, by social science researchers whose arguments required statistical measures in order to gain authenticity. In the 1990s, the census was indirectly impacted by the development in information technology. Often, private players such as consumer goods companies, automobile and fuel industries and service provider consultancies began to produce better and more recent data sets than the census could ever put together in the same time. It is a rather tragic irony of Indian democracy that the enactment of the Citizen's Right to Information coincided with the near obsolescence of the largest data-gathering exercise.

The public admission of the obsolescence of the Census of India, however, came with the NDA government deciding to not conduct the exercise at all. Out goes the baby with the bathwater. Of course, data fudging was not entirely unknown to earlier governments. For instance, the 1971 Census decided 'not to mention' the names of languages which had less than ten thousand speakers, whereas in the 1961 Census, the names of all languages returned by people as their 'mother tongues' were publicised. Marginal adjustment of literacy figures was also not uncommon. However, the NDA government has far surpassed any other government in data-blocking. In order to conceal the large gap between its propaganda and the ground reality, it has resorted to large-scale tailoring of data. The government's record on providing data for debates on economy, welfare, and social composition and gender disparities is unimaginably poor. During the COVID-19 pandemic, it fudged figures of pandemic-related deaths and data on vaccinations till they sprang up from international agencies. The NDA government's decision to abort the 2021 Census, despite not having any viable excuse for doing so, should have caused outrage. That it did not is a testament to the government's success in bringing together the two meanings of the term after a gap of two centuries. The government's promise of marching to the future by taking the country back to the past has been accomplished, in terms of taking away the citizens' right to have a database, however inadequate, that the census once made available.

Going Forward to the Past

THE EVOLUTION OF KNOWLEDGE TRADITIONS NOW perceived globally as 'Western knowledge' has been quite complex, involving countless sub-streams of knowledge drawn from many ancient civilisations as well as modern societies, all woven together into a rationality-based matrix of knowledge developed in modern Europe. The complexity is so much that it would be impossible to trace all of its origins. Yet, at the heart of the entire process was a conception of knowledge as an intellectual outcome, a body of verifiable abstraction. The Western system defines knowledge as a known, as 'logos'. In contrast, Indian traditions of thought—theistic as well as atheistic—looked at knowledge as an experience, as 'knowing' (a verb), an internalised acquisition or, to use a Greek term, as 'gnosis'. The two Sanskrit words *vidya* and *gnyana* correctly represent the basic difference between the two traditions. A verb-based noun phrase can be created in language; but it is not equally true of cultural history. While the Western tradition privileges 'thought' or rationality, the Indian tradition prioritises 'intuition' or the inner ability to perceive. One admits proof and evidence, the other rests upon testimony and truth of word. One attempts to develop methods to turn perception into a logical statement, or theory; the other intensifies the organic link between a pre-existing ocean of wisdom and the consciousness that aspires to open itself to the pre-existent. In simple words, the two are different as material, as cultural deposits and as descriptions of the reality surrounding us. They may intersect, but can hardly fit together in a single arrangement to be used for educating the next generation.

In Indian traditions of learning, memory, described by the term '*smriti*' (meaning 'remembering' as well as 'the remembered'), had been of central interest from the earliest times. The Bhagavad Gita contains a rather categorical pronouncement—*smriti-branshat buddhi-nash*—weakening of *smriti* leads to destruction of the intellect. In ancient theoretical compositions, special care was taken to facilitate the easy remembering of the text by incorporating accessible mnemonic tools, quite akin to those used by Cicero in the Greek tradition. The larger part of ancient Indian literature, belonging to diverse philosophical schools, was preserved through memorisation, with a very high standard of accuracy. There is no other civilisation in the world that showed such obsessive interest in developing memory as the most central tool of learning.

The difference between the turn that the seventeenth-century use of memory took in Europe, resulting in 'universal knowledge', and the traditional use of memory in Indian fields of knowledge, was the idea of a 'science of knowledge', as it emerged in Europe. The Indian idea of knowledge as 'knowing', bringing intellect closer to intuition, together with the sophisticated use of memory for a flawless reproduction of the texts from the past, had resulted in 'apprenticeship' becoming the most favoured mode of receiving and giving education not only in medicine, chemistry, sculpture, architecture, metallurgy, dance, music and crafts, in which skills constitute the major part of understanding, but also in the disciplines in which the ability for abstraction and raising new questions form the core, such as philosophy, poetry, mathematics and astronomy.

As social segregation gained ground within Indian society more than two thousand years ago, the internship mode of cultivating knowledge became a formidable hindrance to the production of a genuine 'universal science'. While highly accurate memorisation continued to be the tool for storing developments in ideas, the access to such memorisation was determined according to the social status of a person. The result was that in pre-colonial times, two broad streams of memory-based knowledge spectrums coexisted, without any possibility for mutual exchange and cross-fertilisation between them: one comprising those who had access to abstract symbols, including writing, and the other comprising of those who were prevented from attempting symbolic abstractions.

This kind of schooling changed after paper became available for use in India during the thirteenth century. However, the place of the oral was not entirely or substantially taken by the written. The two coexisted in an interdependent manner in the Indian production of knowledge. When paper became available, scholars used paper for writing in place of tree bark. Manuscripts were copied meticulously by generations of students and every few hundred years, they were renewed. But there were others who memorised these manuscripts and continued handing down knowledge orally. Therefore, manuscript implied both writing and speech at the same time, and this continued in Indian history for centuries. When print technology arrived in the country, it was not available in every language that had extensive literature, nor did it reach every language that had numerous speakers. It only reached languages spoken by those communities from which the East India Company could recruit bureaucrats and officials. Languages for printing were chosen not on the basis of their literary capabilities or their antiquity, but on the basis of their expediency. Thus, the knowledge traditions that had both oral as well as written forms continued to remain cut off from those that had only the oral form. As a result, the split between the social sections which had easy access to letters and those that were denied this access was aggravated at that precious moment of India's transition from the medieval times to modernity. Thus, the possibility of India devising a grand scheme of classifying all that was known in Indian traditions with the help of a single and unified symbolic grid tied firmly to 'all Indian knowledge'—'all memory'—as had happened a couple of centuries ago in Europe—was made impossible. While Indians had been building houses all along, architecture got divided into 'vernacular' and 'architecture'. Languages, spoken as 'languages', came to be listed differently as 'languages' and 'dialects'. It is with the wound of a deeply divided 'memory field' that India has been trying to internalise the idea of a 'universal knowledge' over the last two centuries.

Now, if an ideology that nurtures the fantasy that 'all knowledge' was developed in ancient India attempts to force educators to bring 'Indian knowledge' to replace 'Western knowledge', it will result in the greatest intellectual disaster known to history. It can at best produce a generation of students who will hold everything in the Western knowledge system in contempt. They will grow up thinking that 'all knowledge' developed in ancient India lies hidden in some manuscript archive. It may even start negating the presence of the great social divide that had kept most castes and all women out of knowledge transactions. At worst, taking India forward to the past will make it a continent of ignorance.

The Future of the Past

HISTORY AS THE PAST AND AS THE REPRESENTATION OF THE past can often, or rather invariably, be at variance. No representation of history can ever capture the entire complexity of all that happened in the past. This is why numerous civilisations have borne witness to the rise of a large variety of writing about the past. These range from hagiographies, mythical accounts of heroes, fantasised depiction of conflicts, vaguely recalled memoirs of large-scale migrations and natural calamities, as well as well-reasoned reproduction of facts, events, lives, regimes and transitions in a people's past. Since the gap between the past and its many representations tends to be specious, a scientific method for history writing was proposed in the nineteenth century. The post-Hegelian understanding of History (as a discipline) is firmly based on the law of causality and veracity. Following its path, a sensible history is expected to say 'x happened because of y circumstances' and support it with evidence drawn from archaeology, texts, archives or testimonies. Departure from either of these principles makes it 'wrong' history—a tendentious representation and a wilful twist given to the past for potential gains in the present. Of course, while the method has clarity, not all of the periods in the past can be well-explained, simply because history (as in, the past) does not take place such that it can be easily transformed into a comprehensive, written 'history' (as in, the representation of the past). Several periods in history do not have enough documents, evidences, testimonies or archives that can be put to use by a historian. Such periods in history become enigmas for future historians, and worse still, they provide room for pushing in myth, legends and imagined 'facts' as 'history'.

During the early part of the twentieth century, when anti-colonial, nationalist movements were gaining strength, wild interpretations of the past, or rather, the imagined past, gained greater currency. A lot of literature in Indian languages around this time drew upon myth for plots and characters. At the same time, some new historical narratives were proposed to support ideologies—some for enhancing equality and freedom, others for justifying inequalities and social division. Dr B.R. Ambedkar's *Annihilation of Caste* (1936) was an interpretation of ancient history in order to analyse the social evils in India. V.D. Savarkar's *Essentials of Hinduism* (1923) and *Bharatiya Itihasatil Saha Soneri Pane* (The Six Golden Pages in India's History), written in his last years, sought to eulogise the 'sanatana' tradition. In the book, Savarkar portrayed Buddhism as an obstruction in the progress of Hinduism. In his works, he depicted the Mughal Empire as an undesirable episode in history. In *Essentials of Hinduism*, he argues that Aurangzeb and Tipu, despite being born of 'Indian' mothers, need to be seen as 'foreigners' and not 'loyal' to India. It is common knowledge that Savarkar regarded Mahatma Gandhi with scorn throughout his life, and was placed in the dock in relation to Gandhi's assassination.

The NCERT's move to purge history texts has its roots in the historiography proposed by Savarkar. The argument that this would 'purify' history of the impact of colonialism and the works of 'leftist historians' is nothing but a convenient argument to cover up the agenda of institutionalising the Hindutva historiography proposed by Savarkar. Since Savarkar's times, an immense body of scholarly works on India's pre-history, proto-history, ancient history, medieval history and modern history has been published by scholars not just from India but also from all over the world. Were one to go to any well-stacked library, one would easily find thousands of books on all aspects of the areas mentioned above. Given the enormous wealth of scholarly works on history, the pressing question is not if the Hindutva view of history is scientific. The question is whether the move will succeed in making any dent in the view of Indian history that universities all over the world have collectively developed through two centuries of scholarship.

The Asiatic Society was founded on 15 January 1784 to study every aspect of the history, religion, languages, culture, society, flora and fauna of what was known then as the Orient. Later, similar institutions inspired by it were founded in London (the Royal Asiatic Society), India (The Asiatic Society of Bombay) and in West Asia. Scholars associated with the Asiatic Society produced a body of studies and translations that became the foundation of knowledge for the nineteenth-century interpretations of Asiatic civilisations. Inspired by it, several colonial scholars took interest in archaeology and history, and brought to light various archaeological deposits, providing the modern world an entry into the ancient civilisations of Asia. Scholars from Asian countries advanced the work of the Orientalists by bringing their knowledge of local languages to aid. From the second half of the nineteenth century, some illustrious institutions of Indology or Oriental studies such as the Baroda Institute for Oriental Studies, Bhandarkar Oriental Institute, Deccan College in Pune and L.D. Institute of Indology in Ahmedabad were set up, furthering knowledge about ancient texts.

Dharmanand Kosambi revived the study of Pali, resulting in the establishment of institutes of study for Pali and Prakrit in West Bengal, Rajasthan and Karnataka. Dravidian studies emerged with the Dravidian Language Family Hypothesis proposed in 1816 by F.W. Ellis (1777–1819). Other illustrious European scholars who contributed to this branch of Asian Studies include Robert Caldwell (1814–1891) and Ferdinand Kittel (1832–1903) during the nineteenth century, and Thomas Burrow, M.B. Emaneau and Kamil Zvelebil during the twentieth century. There is also a long line of Indian scholars who stepped in and further developed the field. Important among them are T.R. Sesha Iyengar (1887–1939) and P.T. Srinivas Iyengar (1863–1931), who were born in the nineteenth century, and Suniti Kumar Chatterjee, Iravati Karve, D.H. Sankalia, Harivallabh Bhayani, Bh. Krishnamoorthy, Iravatham Mahadevan and S. Setter, who were prominent during the second half of the twentieth century.

Throughout the course of the twentieth century, national boundaries of most Asian countries have been redrawn. The narratives of the past and the present of no Asian country can be complete if constructed in isolation from the comprehensive picture that existed earlier. For instance, any body of knowledge about India cannot be complete unless it is seen in the context of India's historical links with countries all over Asia—Syria, Turkey, Iran, Iraq and Afghanistan in the West; China, Uzbekistan, Turkmenistan and Mongolia in the North; and Indonesia, Thailand and Japan in the East. In the last few decades, genetics has contributed much in establishing the routes of prehistoric humans from Africa to Asia and beyond. Archaeology today has advanced non-invasive methods to investigate geological ocean-bed traces of human activities.

Yet, the current worrisome push towards an agenda-bound, aggressive rewriting of history makes it necessary to reassert that the interpretation of the past cannot be made fodder for any vindictive political ideology. During the twentieth century, the world faced a holocaust because pseudo-history was used to sway emotions of the masses towards scorn and hatred. Humanity cannot afford a repetition of that experience today, when the destructive potential of technologies have moved many grades higher. Let us hope that history remains very well secure in its knowledge of the past so that Hindutva's speculative historiography, even when imposed upon learners through the NCERT, can hardly make a dent in it.

The Future of History

IN 1992, A PROVOCATIVE THESIS WAS PUT FORWARD BY THE Japanese-American political scientist Yoshihiro Francis Fukuyama. The book in which it was published had an enigmatic title—*The End of History and the Last Man*. It argued that having won the struggle for a liberal democratic state, humans may not want to go further. They may end up producing banality rather than ideas to transform civilisations in the future. Further, atavistic tendencies may resurface and negate the gains hitherto made. Heroic struggles for equality and freedom may no longer interest the world. As such, the twenty-first century would mark the very end of a uni-dimensional progression of history. Fukuyama's grand curiosity about the future of civilisations led him to speculate whether the progression of humankind from barbarism to liberal democracy leaves humans marooned in banality, instability, atavism and a modern-primitivism.

In the same year that Fukuyama's phenomenal work was published in the US, I was working on a book on literary history in India. My objective was to examine how India has conceptualised its history over the last two millennia. The materials that I gathered for research over a decade made it clear to me that in Indian intellectual traditions—in Sanskrit, Tamil, Pali, Prakrit and modern Indian languages—there did not exist any one way of recollecting the past, which is the appointed business of history. The diversity of perspectives was so striking that I felt compelled to title my work 'Of Many Heroes'. This I had partially drawn from the tenth-century theorist Rajasekhara, who considered the Ramayana as a work with a single hero and the Mahabharata as a work with many heroes. Moreover, determining any single point of origin for the Indian civilisation is too difficult a task. I had in fact forgotten about these intense debates surrounding the beginning of the Indian civilisation, when the issue was brought up again by an announcement from the Central Government's Ministry of Culture. The announcement was about a committee being set up to reconstruct the history of India over the last twelve thousand years. The committee was appointed during the last tenure of the NDA government by the minister Mahesh Sharma. The details of the committee were presented in response to a question raised in the Parliament. A sharp reaction to this disclosure came from the JDS's Coomaraswamy and the DMK's Kanimozhi Karunanidhi; but their criticism was limited to a questioning of the committee's lack of representation of women and South Indians. The basic premise for instituting the committee has, however, not received due attention.

The premise that led to the constituting of this committee forms the heart of the RSS view of India as a nation that holds the Sanatan Vedic tradition of knowledge as non-negotiable.

Every tradition of knowledge offers some profound wisdom and tenable theories. But every aspect of a given knowledge tradition cannot be expected to have eternal validity. Concepts and theories forming a knowledge tradition need to be modified, supplemented and even discarded by future generations in the light of fresh evidence and new discoveries. But, the advocates of Sanatan knowledge do not appreciate criticism levelled against ancient Indian texts in the light of modern knowledge. It does not accept the fact that during the medieval times, many significant saint-poets and thinkers had already gone beyond Vedic texts and modified the 'sacred knowledge' by locating it within the human sphere, which the English language describes as 'secular'. However, any attempt to secularise knowledge is dismissed by the self-proclaimed protectors of Sanatan knowledge by branding it a colonial, Western influence that defiles ancient Indian wisdom.

Since the Vedas were composed in an early variety of the Sanskrit language, this perspective tends to propose an ancestry to the Sanskrit language which is difficult to sustain in the light of available linguistic evidence. The source of the misconception is in one esoteric strand of the nineteenth-century European linguistics. Initially, Sir William Jones had put forward a hypothesis, going by the known similarities between some of the ancient languages, about their origin from a 'proto' Indo-European language. In Jones's hypothesis, 'Indo-Aryan' was used as the name of a language precisely because he wanted to mark it out as distinct from the later-day 'classical' Sanskrit. In an esoteric strand of the nineteenth-century European linguistics, the term 'arya' was interpreted to be the name-tag for a people, which it never was. The term, which meant 'gentleman' or 'respected man' in Sanskrit, was picked up as the slender thread by some Indian scholars inclined towards the idea of a Hindu nation. It was upon this coincidence that the idea of the expedition undertaken to Europe by Sanskrit-speaking ancient Indians in the prehistoric times was built.

No study which is based on a scientific analysis of ancient migrations, archaeology, ancient metallurgy, literary texts, comparative mythology and folklore provides grounds to validate this theory. However, in order to establish the prehistoric and widespread presence of the Sanskrit language, particularly during the third millennium before the Christian era, it becomes necessary at the outset to sort out the unresolved mysteries surrounding the Indus valley civilisation. Its advanced phase is dated, fairly accurately, between 2600 BC and 1900 BC. The date of the composition of the Vedas is widely accepted among serious scholars as falling between 1400 BC and 900 BC. However, these dates, established through elaborate research and careful examination of evidence, are not accepted by Hindutva nationalists. There is a mythological genealogy—a long chain of names of mythical kings—given in the Mahabharata, which is embraced by them as factual 'history'. Quite similarly, they try to establish an imagined account relating to the last ten or more millennia as the factual history of India. Given the ideological moorings of the present government and its eagerness to push its own agenda surrounding the idea of the Indian nation, it would not be far off the mark to expect that the Committee on Indian History has a predetermined mission at hand.

For several millennia, Indians have learnt to live with the idea that there is no single point of origin for the vast diversity of peoples in this subcontinent. A true conceptualisation of the history of the Indian peoples is possible only with the acceptance of multiple origins. Let us hope that the government's committee on history and culture is not designed to merely endorse what the RSS projects as an incontrovertible historical truth. But if it indeed turns out to be so, the future of the history of India may prove Fukuyoma's atavism thesis right.

Past Forward: History, Ideology and the Republic

THE ATTITUDE TOWARDS THE PAST IS ONE OF THE CRUCIAL markers that distinguish a people, nation and civilisation. No two nations or civilisations are likely to have exactly identical ways of perceiving their past. In his essay 'History, Change and Permanence' (1979), sociologist and linguist Madhav Deshpande put forward an insightful hypothesis about India's relation with its past. He pointed out that Indian scholars of ancient texts often tend to project the present onto the past. If some modern ideas were found in an ancient text or practice, it was concluded that everything that is present now was also present in the past. Deshpande argued that in the process of justifying the present by invoking the past, 'often an imaginary past was built to justify the concrete present'. The essay does not discuss fantasy-based claims of 'plastic surgery' on the basis of *Sushrut-Samhita* or aeronautical accomplishments on the basis of *'vimana-vidya'*. Deshpande's comments relate to learned interpretations of the past. His argument is endorsed by several other sociologists. Milton Singer, after studying a community in southern India, observed that the process of osmosis of any cultural experience by Indian communities requires seeking at least a nominal sanction of established traditions. Traditionalising modernity helps, in his view, in giving a ritual status to it. Read together with the *Sankhya* view of time-progression in cycles of a golden era—a *satyayuga* to a degraded *kaliyuga*—these observations may explain why practically every generation in India's post-shastra past of two thousand years has felt that its own time has been a time of steady deterioration. In contrast is imagined some bygone grand era of ethical and social order. This is a view that the material or social view of history may not find rational.

Without overlooking the simplification of a great social complexity, these broad generalisations may help us in understanding why the social discourse in India has always hinged around some perceived imperfection against an imagined perfection in the past. At the popular level, the tension between the two translates into a great sentimental attachment to the past, or an enigmatic longing for things afar—the *para* (the other, alien and distant) and its superlative form *param*, as in *paramartha* or *paramishwara*. The longing in one's heart to escape one's material and tangible world and enter an intangible, other realm or other frameworks of reality imagined to have been in existence in a remote and vague past, is a common pattern of sentiment permeating most social classes and castes in India. For the castes and the classes that faced oppressive exclusion from learning, knowledge, wealth and social status, the desire to escape was but natural. It was equally natural for various social reformers to have wanted to rebel against the exclusion of the oppressed. Since pride of the past—particularly the pride for the imagined 'golden era'—continued to prevail, unhappiness with the present became the hallmark of Indian society until the end of the twentieth century. But a great change has overcome India. The twenty-first century Indian society has no taste for unease with the present, no remorse for being where it is and no desire to escape from the filth of the unethical yuga swabhava which governs it. Indians seem to have decided to celebrate the here and now as the moment of India's rebirth, the nation's self-fulfilment, the moment of having arrived. But that gives rise to a paradox. The idea of a Hindu rashtra is founded on the notion of a punyabhumi, the birthplace of religion. In other words, the Hindutva view cannot exist in isolation from the notion of a past that gave rise to many strands of what is now described in singular as 'Hinduism'. But the supporters of Hindutva, with imagination besieged by constant bombardment of propaganda about the great wealth generated in India in recent years, are asked to think 'positive only'. No complaints of suffering, no disappointment at job losses and no criticism of the government are the habits set to their supplicant minds. Shraddha, bhakti and unquestioning trust are expected of them in order to prove they are not anti-Hindu. Such a citizenry is induced to feel entirely satisfied with what is doled out to it by the dispensation. The real graphs of economic growth may be going south, but if the regime asks them to believe the graphs are rising northward, the *bhakt*-people believe it. They may be rendered jobless, yet the *bhakt*-citizens vehemently believe that India remains at the top of world's prosperity chart. Individual liberties may have sunk way below the constitutional norm, yet they claim that never before have Indians enjoyed so much freedom. They truly believe that India is where it has never been before. That makes the past redundant for them. Thus, the historiography of Hindutva and its idea of the state are at odds with each other. The advocates of Hindutva will have to come up with a solution to this paradox sooner or later. As of now, they continue to have faith in the power of propaganda to conceal every reality.

The rewriting of history textbooks is an attempt to single out those portions that match with Hindutva's view of the past. The others, including Gandhi-ji's assassination, cultural achievements of the Mughal era and the philosophical thought of Buddhism are chopped off as a conspiracy of left-historians, colonial cabal or simply as anti-national fallacies. However, the paradox holds. If the regime is fast turning citizens into unquestioning believers in the regime's magical powers, with chants like '*Modi hai to mumkin hai*' ironing out all scepticism, questions and unhappiness with the present, they shall never want to hark back ruefully to a mythical past. That will make the Hindutva historiography redundant; and without its absurd historiography, the ideology cannot justify driving masses into mass frenzy over a jobless economy as a great growth story. Without its historiography, rampant transgression of the constitution by violent mobs has no rationale. Mythicising history makes people mourn for the present decay. Anaesthetising people's sensitivity to suffering surrounding them takes away their desire to return to history. If that is so, isn't the Hindutva ideology one of the most absurd constructions of the past as well as the present? Does it hope to take the nation forward to the past by wilfully changing history textbooks?

The Bull and the Horse

In the entire discussion related to the Pegasus snooping case and the related political situation in the country, not much attention has been given to the replay of mythology. It is known that Pegasus, the winged sea-horse of Greek mythology, predates by nearly five centuries the famous Trojan horse made for breaching the Ilium citadel of Troy. Horses were in use in ancient Greece in Homer's time, but not much before. They—the horses—spread out from central Asia to Europe around 2000 BC. In contrast, domestication of horses, horse breeding and using horse-driven chariots for warfare became common in India a little later, after the decline of the Harappan civilisation.

The domesticated animal that the Harappans adored was the bull. Bullocks had been domesticated in India at least three millennia prior to the mature phase of the Harappan civilisation, since agriculture had been adopted by a large number of Indians around six thousand years ago. Seals with the humped bull on it were found in excavations of Harappan sites. While the exact time period is unknown, the bull festival had been established in many parts of prehistoric India. Even today, in Maharashtra, Chhattisgarh, Andhra Pradesh and Madhya Pradesh, people celebrate the 'beil-pola' or the bullock felicitation day annually. A prominent name from early history that is associated with bull-based agrarian culture is that of King Bali of tenth century BC. His rule had spread from Rajasthan to the far south and east. Onam in Kerala is celebrated in remembrance of Mahabali or Maveli. It is certain that the bull existed in India much before the breeding and domestication of horses were tried out. During the early Vedic period, India witnessed a clash of civilisations centred on bulls (and cows) and horses, respectively. The conflict was between pastoralists and farmers on the one hand, and warring people and groups associated with fire-sacrifice rituals on the other hand. There are five hymns about the horse in the Rig Veda, but only one about the bull. The story of the Mahabharata provides ample evidence of this clash.

All of this seemingly irrelevant mythological and pre-historic information gains significance today as, in an altogether different case, the same clash has taken centre stage in India. When the farmers in protest had been camping outside Delhi for eight months, the regime remained indifferent to their legitimate demands. Denying the minimum selling price of the farm produce to farmers already under debt traps and a suicide spree, imposing hurriedly passed farm bills favouring corporates, ignoring the striking farmers, placing barriers and nails in their way and farmer deaths during the months of protest are sadly not seen as important issues. Instead, they are branded Khalistani separatists, anti-social mawalis and traitors fattened by funds coming from Canada. In the Marathi language, the term 'Bali-Raja' is used as a symbolic synonym for farmers. Mahatma Jotiba Phule had described Bali as the saviour of the oppressed. During the Dipawali festival, on the day dedicated to cow (vasu-baras), a wishful prayer is recited in every house in Maharashtra: *ida pida talo, baliche rajya yevo* — (may the calamities pass, may the Bali rule return). Indeed, Bali is the ultimate hero for a non-Vedic India. The RSS idea of Hinduism is trained towards going past the Constitution and reviving cultural values and mores of what it thinks was the Vedic culture. This is not to undermine the value of India's intellectual and literary achievements in the early historical times. However, an uncritical glorification of the Vedic culture flies straight in the face of the India that Phule, Periyar and Ambedkar envisioned. The 'past-glory fixation' of the RSS is founded in their self-perception as a people who remained enchained for centuries. It rests on an unchecked fantasy of the Sanskrit-speaking Aryans going all over the world — riding galloping horses — and taking their wisdom to the rest of the known old world. History hardly corroborates this wishful view. The cultural discourse in India today is being pulled in opposite directions by horses and bulls.

Denial of the Past as Historiography

As an agnostic, I am neither a believer nor a non-believer. Yet, there are times when the question of faith gets severely urgent. On Christmas day in 2021, I put aside the book I was reading and switched on the TV to watch news. A debate about the Dharm Sansad in Uttarakhand began to play on screen. One of the participants in it, an audacious champion of Hindu Rashtra, yelled at the anchor: 'Even Shivaji Maharaj had used the term Hindu Rashtra, so what is wrong if I do?' The book that I had been reading was Govind Pansare's *Who Shivaji Was*; and I had just finished reading a letter written in 1657 AD by Shivaji to Aurangzeb appended to the book. The main purpose of the letter was to challenge the infamous zizia tax. Shivaji's anger is directed towards the tax policy and not the religion of Aurangzeb.

Shivaji wrote: 'The government of the Empire is running its daily administration by collecting zizia from Hindus. In fact, formerly, Emperor Akbar ruled with great equanimity.

Therefore, apart from the Daudis and Mohammeds, the religious practices of Hindus such as Brahmins and Shevades (Shaivaites) were protected. The emperor helped these religions. Therefore, he was hailed as a Jagatguru.' The letter goes on to say that Jehangir and Shah Jahan too allowed undisturbed practice of all religions: 'Those Emperors had always their eyes fixed on people's welfare.' Shivaji contrasts those three emperors with Aurangzeb and warns him: 'Under your rule, you have lost many forts and provinces. The rest are also likely to be lost. This is because you do not spare in doing everything that is base.' I am aware that the present dispensation will not approve of Shivaji Maharaj's analysis that Akbar was called Jagatguru by the people because he protected everyone irrespective of their religion. In fact, those who assassinated Govind Panasare in 2015 disapproved of his description of Shivaji as a ruler interested in the welfare of all, irrespective of religion.

Shivaji even questions Aurangzeb's understanding of the Quran. He writes in the letter, 'The Quran is a heavenly book. It is God's utterance. It commands that God belongs to all Musalmans and, infact, the entire world.' He adds, 'In masjids, it is He who is prayed. In temples, it is He for whom the bells are tolled. To oppose anyone's religion is like forsaking one's own religion. It is wiping out what God wrote; it is to blame God Himself.' Since I had read these lines just minutes ago, I did not know whether to laugh at the ignorance of the person yelling on TV or feel sad at such a demeaning distortion of Shivaji's idea of Hindu culture.

Just the day before Christmas, the Karnataka Assembly had brought in the anti-conversion bill; and on the night of 25 December an image of Jesus was desecrated by vandals in Ambala. A day later, the news of the Ministry of Home

Affairs blocking the FCRA for Mother Teresa's organisation hit headlines in newspapers the world over. In the backdrop of the Karnataka anti-conversion bill, euphemistically called the Protection of Religious Rights Bill, the Hindutva propaganda machinery had been spreading fake news about the rise in the population of Christians. As per census data, Christians in Karnataka were 1.91 per cent of the total population in 2001. A decade later, in 2011, they were 1.87 per cent, slightly lesser than before. However, another website comes up when one searches for the census data for Christians in Karnataka on the internet. Its masthead displays the image of the legislative assembly building in Bangalore, passing it off for a government website. It shows the Christian population as being 3.1 per cent. An internet search reveals that the website is put up by the founder of a digital media set-up which had handled Narendra Modi's election campaign in 2014. As if the intimidation and assaults on Christians and the warning of genocide hurled at Muslims in the recent dharm-sansads were not enough, there was, a month ago, the terrifying formulation by NSA Ajit Doval that the fourth-generation wars will be waged through civil society.

Recent events leave no room of doubt as to the nature of Hindutva that is being promoted in thought and action. This Hindutva ideology is trying hard to establish that Hinduism is not the tolerant co-existence of faiths as Shivaji interpreted it in his times, or a way of life that will recite names of Ishwar and Allah as essentially the same. Going by the articulation of violence sought to be unleashed by the dharma-sansads within Indian society and the semi-official theorising of civil society as a weaponry planted by the enemy, it is clear that Narendra Modi's vishvaguru-nation fantasy is poles apart from Shivaji's idea of a jagatguru-ruler who professes no dharma but the raj-dharma.

The RSS ideology of Hindutva, apart from being militaristic, has an obsession with a tendentious historiography. This historiography is so wishful that it sets aside all established scientific methods of reading the past and brings in untenable and wild pronouncements as historical truth. The rivalry that Hindutva historiography has cultivated with scientific representation of the past resurfaced recently in an IIT calendar. On 18 December 2021, IIT Kharagpur released a calendar for 2022. Its aim was to 'recover the foundations of Indian Knowledge Systems'. That sounds good on the face of it. But what it managed to do is to present an unscientific narrative of India's prehistory. It hitched together two entirely unrelated postulates. One relates to the question of the origin and spread of the Sanskrit language, the other relates to the Indus valley civilisation which precedes the arrival of Sanskrit in India. It also brought in the frame Adolf Hitler, without forgetting to mention that Hitler was 'elected to power'. It asserted that the Vedic civilisation is the alpha and the omega of Indian civilisation. The concocted historical narrative and militant view of religion make this loud brand of Hindutva go against all that the Indian traditions of thought and spirituality hold precious, as reflected in Buddha and Basaveshwar, in Kabir and Gandhi, in Charvaka and Ambedkar. Besides, quite worryingly, the ideas of Muslim genocide and harassment of Christians are against the Constitution and the law of the land, even as they form a part of Hindutva.

Of Many Heroes

'WE ARE UNAWARE OF THE BEGINNING AND THE END OF the world; the first and the last pages of this old book have fallen off.' This epigram comes from Abu Talib Kalim, an important figure in India's literary history, though quite forgotten in the present. Born at Hamadan in Iran in 1585, he felt drawn to India and arrived in Bijapur five centuries ago, in 1621, going on to live in India till his death in 1651. During these years, he produced nearly twenty-four thousand verse couplets, distinguished by their pithy wisdom. I was drawn to his witty couplet on history around thirty years ago when I was working on India's literary history. The title of my book was *Of Many Heroes*. I chose Kalim's lines as its epigraph.

The title of my book was drawn from a line in the *Kavyamimansa* by Rajashekhara, a tenth-century poet, dramatist and scholar. He worked in the court of the Pratihara kings in Gujarat. While pointing to the difference between the Ramayana and the Mahabharata, Rajashekhara had commented that while poetry can have a single hero, history has to have many heroes. Therefore, I titled my book

Of Many Heroes. Rajashekhara, living during the ninth and tenth centuries, wrote in Sanskrit and Prakrit. Abu Talib Kalim, in the sixteenth to seventeenth centuries, wrote in Persian. Despite being separated by seven centuries and hailing from different linguistic and religious traditions, the two distinguished Indian poets had a shared view on Indian history. They both knew that for any authentic representation of India — historical or literary — one must think in terms of the many origins of this civilisation, in terms of diversity rather than a forced superficial unity.

When I was working on my book in 1990-91, I was not as acutely aware as I am now that the question of history may later assume a disproportionately high centrality to the political discourse in India. As I look back at the arguments and debates during the last quarter century, the replacement of old myths by new myths, old deification by new deification, and displacement of logic by wishful reconstruction of the past, I notice that the element of diversity inherent in India's past has been deliberately overlooked. It seems that the creativity in grasping India's being displayed during freedom struggle and the insights that the poets and thinkers of the medieval ages brought to bear upon the social discourse have hit a parched course. The struggle for independence in India was also to some extent a struggle for decolonising our minds. M.K. Gandhi's *Hind Swaraj* (1909) is its most articulate statement. Our freedom struggle was simultaneously a struggle to create a new nation with a humane society that would uphold the principles of equality and dignity of every individual. B.R. Ambedkar's *Annihilation of Caste* (1936) is the most passionate plea to bring about this transformation in India. In some sense, the two founding fathers of India had indicated between them, how it would be necessary to reject the baggage imposed by the West in the name of modernity and by the past in the name of a superficially united nation. During the post-Gandhi-Ambedkar era in India, their ideas were gradually turned into nothing more than ritualistic memory.

The rejection of the oppressive West came to be seen as an unquestioning adherence to the past, and the freedom from the oppressive past came to be seen as alienation from the past, together with an unmatched enthusiasm for imbibing the West. This has reduced the India of today to a society devoid of any central vision, an idea that will free us and enable us to move forward in time. We are caught between the tyranny of a reductive nationalism and a coercive vision of a unified past. Acceptance of diversity may help us in going beyond the reactionary tendencies of the present. Diversity can be a useful ideal for deepening our democracy, securing our biodiversity and cultural plurality, and for setting right our perspectives on politics, culture and history. Federalism needs to be the guiding star of our public discourse, and the identity marker 'India, a union of states' in our Constitution is its most iconic statement.

In recent times, three issues which could not be more removed from the daily lives of Indians are being given undue importance. First among these is the place of Sanskrit in the making of the Indian civilisation. The RSS-inspired history likes to place Sanskrit as the origin of all knowledge and culture in our past, despite the fact that knowledge traditions in India have emerged from Pali, Prakrit and Dravidic as well. Human inhabitants of the subcontinent used other languages prior to the emergence of Sanskrit and those languages found continuation in the form of Pali, Prakrit and ancient Tamil. Sanskrit brought to ancient India a different world view, memory tradition and social structure. There were active exchanges among the languages existing in the subcontinent. Yet, the RSS insists that all other languages were derived from Sanskrit and that even during the Indus civilisation it was Sanskrit that dominated thought and life. No existing science, linguistics, genetics, archaeology or history corroborates this position. Yet, the reductive nationalism persists, relying on flawed linguistics and archaeology.

Another folly of the RSS is its perception of the medieval ages in Indian history as the era of 'invasion' and 'cultural destruction'. It is true that these centuries mark the contact with Islam in Indian history. However, it is also true that the exchanges and trade with the countries to the west of India, from Afghanistan to Turkey, has been a phenomenon ever since humans have inhabited Asia. Besides, what is seen as 'destructive invasion' was in reality a time of new synthesis in arts, literature, ideas, architecture, law, medicine and theological views. All of that is deliberately demonised and brushed aside, for Islam provides the most convenient 'enemy' metaphor for Hindu nationalism to prosper.

The third misconception that has gained ground is the nature of the freedom struggle, its major protagonists and their life histories. The BJP's propaganda machine has been deliberately portraying that discord existed among Gandhi, Patel, Subhash Bose, Tagore, Nehru, Ambedkar and Maulana Abul Kalam Azad. False information is being mercilessly peddled, making them look like erring men of public affairs—selfish, pretentious and unmindful of what is good for India. The scale of this misinformation is such that it seems impossible to counter.

However, in the future, when India recovers from this assault on its history and culture, these flawed arguments and the tendentious history presented through them are bound to look deliberate and short-sighted. India of a single origin, a single linguistic and cultural mould, with only one kind of people, adhering to only one religion would be a far cry from its identity over several millennia. Linguistic, cultural and social diversity is its definitive identity marker. India can continue to be a nation only so long as we perceive it as a 'union of states'.

Educating India to Return to the Past

THE ANNOUNCEMENT OF THE NATIONAL EDUCATION Policy sent a wave of despondency across the academic community in the country. The hollowness of the policy was evident in its complete unwillingness to address the question of caste, gender and equality. Will the proposed education help the society become less caste-tormented? Will it reduce the class divide? Will it cure us of the great gender divide which has remained the bane of education in India all along? The policy had no answers to these pressing questions. Probably, the active promotion of the view that the state is not obliged to protect education from becoming a service-market will leave the Indian society even more socially and economically fragmented than it already is.

Several elements of the policy made it look more like a set of pipe-dreams rather than a plan based on a sound understanding of the needs of the stakeholders. But the most striking aspect was its lack of insight into the history of modern education in India since the establishment of the first three universities 170 years ago. It was a time when universities were responsible merely of conducting examinations and providing certification to the matriculating and graduating students. The responsibility of teaching was left to high-schools and colleges. Through a long process spanning decades, efficient regulators were put in place to ensure the responsibility of teaching as well as certification were not abdicated in the face of caste and communal pressures. The regulators too went through a long process of evolution and, over time, adapted themselves to the provisions in the Constitution that had struck a fine balance between the Centre and the states in the matter of education. The new policy overlooks the entire history of education in modern India and seeks to reinvent the wheel all over again. One can only imagine the scale of confusion and misconduct arising during the transition, particularly since the number of colleges expected to line up for 'autonomy' is phenomenally large now. Larger still is the number of institutions of technical education.

The language perspective spelt out in the policy begs criticism and fundamental disagreement. The three-language policy that worked during the 1960s can no longer serve the needs of the complex demographic reality of present-day India, far less that of the future. Invariably, the cities with a population above 20 lakh have become linguistically far complex than ever before in history, and would require nothing less than an enlightened 'multilingual education'. Every educationist knows that multilingual education does not stop at offering an option in either the medium of education or choosing the language subjects. Promoting Sanskrit is as necessary as promoting the study of Japanese, Chinese and Russian; but promoting it at the cost of some of the scheduled languages in India such as Tamil, Kannada, Marathi and Bangla can cumulatively lead to a growing tension between Hindi speakers and the speakers of languages other than Hindi. Children studying in schools in Hindi-speaking states are more likely to opt for Sanskrit as the optional or additional language; and those studying elsewhere are likely to move to foreign languages. A much more flexible multilingualism could have helped in avoiding, in the first place, this fault-line from taking shape.

The insane desire to replace everything Western with Indian may pass off as patriotism, but in reality, it is pseudo-nationalistic jingoism; but since that is philosophically unviable, the attempt may leave the learners pathetically partial in their understanding of the world.

Though not stated explicitly in the document, there are clear indications that the policy aims for a shift in the knowledge paradigm. Academic institutions are concerned about the impending spectre of having to move from a well-established order of universal knowledge to a paradigm of knowledge drawn from ancient Indian sources. What has been approved as yet by the cabinet is just the policy. Its implementation in full measure is likely to take several years. One does not know if, once implemented, it will remain true to the spirit of the policy. But, assuming that it does, what may unfold before us may have the scale of a cultural revolution aiming at 'purifying' minds, resulting in a radical social engineering. However, the transition from the prevailing order of universal knowledge to any brand of 'Indian' knowledge will require tackling a complex legacy of philosophical impossibilities. Neither the realm of the universal knowledge, nor the realm of any tradition of knowledge in India is constituted in a way that makes one compatible with the other.

A major difficulty in attempting a comparative study of the Western and Indian knowledge paradigms is that the meanings of the concepts that form the building blocks of knowledge are not exactly identical in the two traditions. The terms 'gnosis', 'logos' and 'philosophy' used in the West are translated in many Indian languages as 'jnana', 'vidya' and 'darshan'. 'Philosophy', for instance, refers to a perspective for approaching a set of questions and a logical framework used for understanding phenomena such as existence, universe, knowledge and reason. On the other hand, 'darshan', the Sanskrit for 'a school' or 'a grand theory', is closer to vision or the process of viewing rather than the view itself. The difficulty is further compounded by the continuous shift every few centuries, in both paradigms, in the semantic associations constituting these terms. For instance, 'Veda', initially meaning 'knowledge', began to indicate 'articulation of knowledge' towards the end of the Vedic period.

Ever since the modern West came in contact with India, Western scholars have produced a vast amount of literature on Indian culture and traditions. Friedrich Max Müller *The Sacred Books of the East* (1879–1910), for instance, was quite generous in complimenting the wisdom found in ancient literature. However, the overwhelming majority of European administrators, scholars and researchers of his time had internalised the idea that British rule was necessary for 'civilising India', a divinely ordained duty they had accepted as a moral burden.

These views, whether negative or superlative, inevitably influenced the self-image of Indian thinkers of the time. Consequently, there was great excitement and acceptance of the colonial policy of English education throughout the nineteenth century. This was accompanied by a dismissal of

Indian forms of knowledge by the native literary class in India. Yet, despite being culturally irrelevant, that body of knowledge has by now become the core substance in Indian education. This may be described as unfortunate; yet, any attempt to replace this body of knowledge at this stage in India's history is bound to lead to an equally unfortunate situation.

Countries such as Ireland, Canada and Australia also had to fight the Western disapproval of their indigenous knowledge systems. Though the impact of colonialism can be justifiably held responsible for India's disproportionately low contribution to 'knowledge' during the last two centuries, focusing on colonialism alone may not perhaps yield the complete story of our failure. In order to get a complete picture, one must turn to the text of a lecture that B.R. Ambedkar — a formidable scholar, mass leader and the architect of free India's Constitution — was to, but could not, deliver at Lahore and which was published in the form of a book under the title *Annihilation of Caste* (1936). There is no doubt that the caste discrimination in the past as well as the present, apart from colonial cultural domination and the continued 'knowledge imperialism' of the West, have had their share in reducing 'knowledge' in India to pauperisation and 'education' in India to a savage mockery of the idea of learning. Sadly, what has been brought in as the National Education Policy overlooks all these cultural references and instead, presents the nation a future clouded by steps that will take us back into history, alas.

Anti-Science Regime:
An Intelligent Design?

OF THE MANY PUBLICATIONS OF CHARLES DARWIN, WHO died more than a hundred and forty years ago, two are most well known. The first was based on a long voyage he undertook on the *HMS Beagle* as a young naturalist of twenty-two years. His diary of 770 pages was published as a journal under the title *Journal of Researches into the Geology and Natural History of the Various Countries Visited by H.M.S. Beagle* (1839). This created a reputation for him as a cutting-edge naturalist. Though he had almost settled on the theory of evolution by the early 1840s, he kept postponing the publication of his most important work until he came to know that another naturalist was about to publish a somewhat similar theory. So, in 1859, at the age of fifty, Charles Darwin published *On the Origin of Species by Means of Natural Selection, or the Preservation of Favoured Races in the Struggle for Life*. This was as important a publication in the entire history of science as was Newton's *Philosophiae Naturalis Principia Mathematica* (1687). It forever changed the perception surrounding the evolution of the animal and plant species as radically as Newton's treatise changed the perception of matter and motion. In his later years, Darwin wrote his autobiography, primarily for his children and grandchildren. Between Isaac Newton and Charles Darwin, they had managed to reduce the status of the scriptural accounts of the cosmos and life to be pure myth and blind belief. Darwin was aware of the wrath of the Church that his scientific thesis invited. Therefore, in the autobiography, he described himself as an agnostic. After his death in 1882, when the question of his burial came up, the ecclesiastical authorities in England allowed for his burial at the Westminster Abbey with full pomp, much to the credit of the Anglican Church. However, consent for Darwin's burial did not automatically stop the spread of anti-evolutionary ideas.

In the United States of America, pitched court-room battles had to be fought for getting schools to accept Darwinism. Historically, the most important among these was the case that school-teacher John Scopes fought in 1925 against the ban on Darwin from school curriculum in several states. Orthodoxy remained unmatched in the US over the next four decades until the 1960s, when the Supreme Court decided against teaching the mythology of creation as science. However, Darwin's theory did not have an entirely smooth sailing even after this legal success. The year 1984 saw the publication of *The Mystery of Life's Origin: Reassessing Current Theories*, co-written by the creationist and chemist Charles B. Thaxton. Since then, the idea of an 'intelligent design' has prompted pseudo-scientists to promote the view that the complexity and diversity of species is far too overwhelming to allow a simple Darwinian formula of evolution and natural selection. This too has been argued in American courts. In 2005, the district judge of Dover, John Jones ruled that the 'intelligent design' is a merely religious argument. He reminded the petitioner Kitzmiller that the Supreme Court of US had made it unconstitutional to teach 'creation science' (the Biblical myth of genesis) in public schools.

India has now joined the debate. The NCERT recently decided to keep Darwin out of school texts. It is surprising as to why teachers of science in schools and lecturers in science colleges have not tendered resignations in protest. Does it mean they are no more than mere 'science labourers' rather than being scientists? Some courageous scientists did protest; but will the government that showed no sensitivity to lakhs of farmers who sat on dharna for a year, pay heed to protesting scientists? Article 51 (A) of the Constitution has laid down 'fostering scientific temper' as a directive principle, but it does not define what scientific temper is. A parallel example of the 'intelligent design' thesis in the Indian context would be the *Purusha Sukta* of Rig Veda and its ham-handed successor *Manusmriti*. The *Purusha Sukta* describes the Purusha, the universe (of whom are born the *rig* and the *saman*—the Vedas), and later the horses, and other animals such as goats and sheep. The Purusha was divided by the gods. From the mouth of the divided Purusha came the Brahmin; from the arms came the Rajanya; from the thighs came the Vaishya; and from the feet came the Shudra. Genesis myths of this kind mark early literature, particularly the literature that is seen as scriptural, in every civilisation. In the oral literature of tribal communities in India, we come across a variety of such creation myths about the rise of the human species, assigned with the moral responsibility to keep the universe going.

Every religion is based on its unique genesis story, and every culture or nation finds it nourishing to have its own version of how or where it began in some mythical time. Some claim to have emerged from the sun; others claim their origin in the moon; yet others in some distant ocean, or a mythical mountain or forest. What is astounding is that, in ancient India, the story of genesis was used as a basis for laws governing inter-community relations. The hierarchy of the vocationally high and low implied in the *Purusha Sukta* of the Rig Veda was taken to mean a prescription with legal sanction. Thus, any attempt in thought, move or gesture to change the hierarchy came to be seen as a sin against Purusha. Later, at whatever date the *Manusmriti* came into circulation, Purusha of the Rig Veda was replaced by Brahma, a deity with whom Vedic lore would not have felt at ease.

If such myths regarding the emergence of the cosmos come to be positioned as the 'intelligent design' proposed by India in the remote past, and if these myths are pressed into the vacuum created by shunting Darwinism out, modern India can be freed from its Constitution and delivered straight into the hands of the *Manusmriti*—rebranded as the 'Saffron Book', a la, the *Red Book* in China. Even a cursory reading of B.R. Ambedkar's *Who Were the Shudras?* can show how utterly nonsensical the formulation of *Manusmriti* was. But leaving aside the question of its implications for the Constitution and its directive principles, let us remember that as per the latest numbers (since reliable data is on a sabbatical), India had twenty-two thousand science colleges, over a thousand universities with various science departments and nearly sixty thousand doctoral scholars in the science stream. If they are required to discard Darwinism as an insult to India's cultural past, to what great intellectual future is this entirely anti-science government taking them? NCERT's dropping Darwin out of the textbooks is, in my opinion, a suicidal aberration without parallel in modern India's history.

Scholars Stand Up for Reason

It is impossible to decide if Time at all exists or if it is not but an imagined absolute. Leaving aside the metaphysical uncertainty, it is necessary to accept that human affairs carry upon them a deep imprint of the unceasing interplay between the past and the present of individuals, families, societies and nations. Depending on the material, cultural and ideological expediencies of a given present, societies and nations conceptualise, constitute, inhabit and represent their past—or rather, their numerous, continuously shifting pasts. Always in the process of getting restructured, no single version of the past can withstand the test of absolute authenticity. The openness of history as a field of enquiry allows autocratic regimes and class hegemony to replace historical narratives with irrational and untenable claims. They tend to raise the pitch of hatred against the ancestors of those people against whom revenge is sought to be invoked. In order to bolster up the self perception of the dominant sections of society, such regimes concoct illusions of a glorious past—framing them as the essential identity of the people—no matter how far such claims are from the truth of history. Today's India is a living example of this pattern of re-imagining history, wilfully brought to depart from its rational confines.

A Press Bureau of India (PBI) post dated 14 September 2020 reported that an expert committee had been constituted by the government for 'conducting holistic study of origin and evolution of Indian culture since 12000 years to present'. A similar committee was appointed earlier in 2017 when Mahesh Sharma was the Minister of Culture, with a similar representation. There was no woman member in it; none from the north-east; only one member from the South; no SC/ST scholars; and none at all who were not Hindus. The composition raises serious concerns about the nature of the mission. A Reuters report by Rupam Jain and Tom Lasseter dated 6 March 2018 attempted to lay bare the intentions of the 2017 committee. Reuters reviewed the minutes of the committee's meetings and held interviews with committee members, and set out the following to be its aims: 'to use evidence such as archaeological finds and DNA to prove that today's Hindus are directly descended from the land's first inhabitants many thousands of years ago, and make the case that ancient Hindu scriptures are fact, not myth'. Minister Mahesh Sharma told Reuters that 'he expects the conclusions of the committee to find their way into school textbooks and academic research'. The two sciences on the basis of which the Ministry of Culture is trying to recast the Indian past are genetics and archaeology. The RSS has made itself an expert in circulating random selections of partially verified findings drawn from these two disciplines to support its predetermined conclusions. The scientific community were agitated by the spread of such spurious claims.

In September 2019, David Reich of Harvard and many other scientists from some of the most respected universities published in *Science* a paper proving that the emergence of the Sanskrit language does not predate the Indus civilisation. The paper claims that the language came to India with the people from the Eurasian steppes, centuries after the Indus civilisation declined. In contrast, the RSS historiography aims to assert that the Sanskrit-speaking Indian Aryans ventured out to other parts of the world. This hypothesis has no backing either in archaeology or in genetics. This is, in fact, not the only instance when scientists felt agitated by the anti-scientific claims of Hindutva historiography. In June 2022, a media report stated that the Ministry of Culture had funded genetic verification of 'pure' communities. The proposal, bringing back to memory the horrifying Nazi Eugenics, made the scientific community immediately react in anguish. Within days, they wrote an open letter to the ministry, with more than a hundred signatories to it. The signatories included eminent professors from the country's leading scientific and technology institutes.

Ever since I learnt about the official plans of creating a wishful history, I thought of forming an informal collective of scholars to prepare a scientifically conceived, comprehensive and coherent report on the embattled past. After spending three years contacting some of the most outstanding archaeologists and historians, along with reputed institutions of archaeology, Indology and South Asian studies around the world, my idea began to materialise. The field is vast, the weave of intellectual traditions in the disciplines is complex and the challenges involved are far too many, to say the least. To work on such a project without institutional support, secretarial assistance and under a strict deadline was nothing short of madness. I persisted, however, being acutely aware that to restore reason is the need of the hour. I am glad I did. Several hundred scholars from some of the best universities and institutions evinced keen interest in the project. Eighty-eight of them joined hands to write the proposed report. It covers a very large temporal span, beginning with the arrival of *homo sapiens* in South Asia and ending with the onset of the third millennium. It discusses continuities as well as discontinuities in India's past and presents a comprehensive picture of population migrations, emergence of social and political organisations, development of philosophies and metaphysics, the diversity of languages and expression, major social movements, impact of colonialism on Indian ideas and culture, the freedom struggle and the making of India since Independence. It is conceptualised to provide adequate space for the histories of various regions, faiths and languages.

In India's history, the timelines of social transformation vary from region to region. Distinct 'periods' did not begin simultaneously in all parts of India. While one region moved ahead, many other areas in the subcontinent continued their existence in 'another time'. In India, many eras continue to co-exist in any cultural practice and social system. The report focuses on the people of India rather than on kingdoms. The contributors to the report have impressively diverse profiles, making it sufficiently inclusive. The 600-page report on the Civilisation and Histories of India was publicly announced on 9 October 2022 in a meeting of scholars in Delhi. Ideally a work in progress, it needs to be repeatedly refined and revised, so that no extreme stand ever gains ground and gets translated into acts or thoughts which may diminish the Constitution that makes India—Bharat—a union of traditions, transformations and people.

Is India Being Pushed into Knowledge Isolation?

One of the recurring themes in the BJP government's discourse is that of making India 'vishwaguru'. The government's policy for education, its restructuring of higher education regulators, its wishful depiction of ancient India's past and its cultural politics—all are oriented towards claiming for India the status of a 'knowledge-country'. On the face of it, the idea sounds alluring; but it cannot be accomplished through self-glorification or through mere propaganda. Unless the deep incompatibility between the Sanskrit universe of knowledge and the 'universal knowledge' by which the world lives is understood, all adventurist steps taken are likely to result in the exact opposite of what is desired. And in the process, India may be pushed into becoming an anti-knowledge nation.

Throughout human history, man has attempted to understand the universe by using various ingenious methods of encrypting its formal and material features. From the ancient Egyptian hieroglyphs and Greek trigonometry to the medieval European magical-code languages, these methods had essentially aimed at storing human experiences in ways that would make them 'transferable', giving them existence beyond their natural life. The desire to represent, store, transact and pass on to the succeeding generations what humans 'know', culminated in the seventeenth-century French thinker Leibniz's conceptualisation of a 'pure language', a language of signs that do not have meaning in themselves but have the ability to represent constant and entirely non-subjective meanings. During the transition from the use of Latin to modern European languages for intellectual and imaginative expression—in the seventeenth century—the obsession to invent a symbolic method for 'stating knowledge' made it possible for European scholars to arrive at sorting ideas in terms of what came to be accepted as 'universal science'. Earlier, in 1582, Giordano Bruno had come up with the idea that combining 'associations of ideas' in manageable symbolic strings would help holding a vast amount of knowledge in a relatively small band of human memory. A century later, in 1675, Leibniz proposed his celebrated 'logical calculi', stated in the aphorism *'existere nihil aliud esse quam harmonicum esse'* (to exist is nothing other than to be harmonious). In that span of a century and a half from Bruno to Leibniz, Europe had discovered the ability of the human mind to reduce diverse perceptions to a 'harmonised understanding', capable of being stated in abstract terms. This ability is described in philosophical terms as 'rationality'. If René Déscartes (1595–1650) gave to Europe the philosophical basis for its rationality, often highlighted through his claim *'je pense, donc je suis'* (I am, because I think), Bruno, Leibniz and their contemporaries gave Europe the 'method' of stabilising knowledge on the bedrock of rationality. The history of 'sorting out and storing ideas' in Europe should be of interest to India as well, for, in the process, memory started getting transmuted from being just a commonly shared heritage of human societies to a higher order platform for commanding and canonising the cerebral acts of humans, resulting in the idea of a 'universal knowledge', which is the real business of universities.

These historical factors would not be relevant to the analysis of the trajectory of 'knowledge' in India, if they did not clearly point to the use of memory for encrypting and classifying knowledge. In Indian traditions of learning, memory had been a central interest from the earliest times. In fact, what was worth learning was described with the term 'smriti' ('remembering' as well as 'the remembered'). The Bhagavad Gita states rather categorically that weakening of 'smriti' leads to destruction of the intellect—*smriti-branshat buddhi-nash*. In ancient literature and theoretical compositions, special care was taken to facilitate easy remembering of the text by introducing various accessible mnemonic tools, quite akin to the Ciceronean use of memory. Rarely has another civilisation in the world focused on developing natural memory as the most central tool of learning as India did for millennia.

However, the fundamental difference between the turn that the seventeenth-century use of memory took in Europe and the fixation with memory in India was that here, the idea of a 'science of knowledge' or a 'universal knowledge' did not find favour with those who were expected to cultivate knowledge. The idea of knowledge as 'knowing', bringing in a subjective intuition as the horizon of intellect, together with the seasoned use of memory for a flawless reproduction of the texts from the past, had resulted in 'guru-parmapara' and 'apprenticeship' becoming the privileged mode of education in India. This was a challenge. It became even more menacing when combined with the stringent gender and caste segregation that besieged the Indian society more than two thousand years ago. The gender-exclusionary and clan or caste-based apprenticeship mode of knowledge transmission became a formidable hindrance in producing any genuine 'universal science'. While high-accuracy memorisation continued to be the tool for storing developments in ideas, the access to such memorisation was restricted according to the caste origin of the learners. During precolonial times, two broad streams of memory-based knowledge emerged in India without the possibility for mutual exchange and cross-fertilisation: one, the memory traditions of those with access to abstract symbols, including writing; and two, the memory traditions of those who were denied symbolic abstractions. The latter continued as 'knowledge-workers' within their limited confines. The possibility of India devising a grand scheme of classifying 'all that was known' in the diverse knowledge traditions with the help of a single and unified symbolic grid—'all memory'—did not take shape.

It is with the wound of a deeply divided 'memory field' that India has been trying to internalise the idea of a 'universal knowledge' over the last two centuries. The nineteenth-century attempts to modernise society had to launch upon the project of creating access to a shared band of abstract signs, opening transition to new fields of knowledge that qualified to be 'universal' science. Similar, perhaps far more difficult, was the struggle to get girls into formal education. After a century and a half of that difficult struggle, the BJP education policy is trying to prioritise and privilege the 'sanatan vidyas', and coaxing scientists to revisit long forgotten theories, giving them preference over what is described in the RSS terminology as 'the pollution caused by Western knowledge'. The sheepish Vice Chancellors and boards of studies are propagating the mood in order to safeguard their funding. If the project succeeds, we may soon find ourselves become an anti-knowledge nation. If the education policy imposed on universities asks for an unquestioning acceptance of all that was ancient, the result will be a fatal loss of the ability to ask meaningful questions, the primary task for which universities exist.

The Question of Questioning

Democracy is not just about 'being' a system and how a nation is organised. It is more about its continuous 'becoming', inclusive of and accountable to those who constitute the nation. One of the important indicators of vibrancy of a democracy is the freedom of media in it, something as important as breath to a living body. While it is not a vital organ of the state in itself, its absence can leave the body inert. Two recent reports indicate that media in India is gasping for breath.

The Press Freedom Report (PFR) put out by 'Reporters without Borders' has India ranked 142nd out of 180 countries covered in 2020, and 140th in 2019. It observes that globally, there is a 'crisis caused by growing hostility and even hatred towards journalists'. Placing Brazil of Bolsonaro at the 102nd rank and the USA of Donald Trump at the 45th rank, it points out that the two leaders 'continue to denigrate the media and encourage hatred of journalists in their respective countries'. While the PFR presents a comparative global view of media, *Getting Away with Murder* by Geeta Seshu and Urvik Sarkar looks specifically at the situation in India. It points out that thirty-six instances of attack on media persons took place during 2019, and 198 between 2014 and 2019. One in every five attacks involved murder. The increasing frequency of such attacks is alarming. Almost invariably, the perpetrators have not been punished. Most cases have not moved past the FIR stage and only a few have reached court trial. The report records that the perpetrators of the attacks included 'government agencies, security forces, political party members, religious sects, student groups, criminal gangs and local mafias'.

Media has now become a dangerous occupation. The hazards include physical attacks, threats and trolling in the foulest language, mental torture and lack of adequate legal relief. In such a situation, how can the nation expect the media to speak up when it is expected to? The Constitution does promise freedom of expression as a fundamental right; but it is subject to 'reasonable restrictions' — an expression that the regime seems to have left to a spacious interpretation. In addition to the Prevention of Terrorism Act (PoTA), the Unlawful Activities (Prevention) Act (UAPA) and the century-old Official Secrets Act in force since 1923, other regulations too are being used now to target inconvenient media houses, journalists, cartoonists, writers, film-makers, cinema artists, dramatists, publishers and information activists. Law, which ideally should defend the independence of journalism, is being used to silence it, in addition to various extra-legal methods. If any courageous TV or print journalist raises questions, they are trolled relentlessly. Look at Anand Teltumbde and Gautam Navlakha, for instance. In an ideal democracy, they should have received something similar to the Pulitzer to honour their courage and depth in writing. What they have received, instead, is arrest by the

National Investigation Agency (NIA). Extending adequate constitutional and legal protection to scribes and questioners could be wished, had wishes been horses! This wish is quickly dashed by inscrutable delay in criminal investigation and python-slow court procedures. Asha Rajdeo Ranjan has yet been making futile rounds of CBI courts to get to the book the killers of her husband, a bureau chief in *Hindustan Times* who was murdered in 2016. One cannot easily forget, alas, that a female court employee who charged a mighty judge with sexual harassment was sacked and her case was heard and dismissed by the very same judge. Is gagging questioners the new normal in India?

In 2020, Supriya Sharma of *Scroll.in* who wrote a story about shortages in food supply—a humdrum journalistic task, really—had to face an FIR. The report was not just about one of the seven lakh nondescript villages where migrant labourers returned to and languished after the lockdown. The report related to the Prime Minister's parliamentary constituency. Staring before her was the almost certain reward of a jail term. Given the sorry state of those who raise questions and the hazards created for media as a profession, is it surprising that the media and media persons lie supine? Yet, intimidation by those in power is not entirely new for media. What is new is the threat posed to it by a fraudulent competitor—fake news. Bolsonaro and Trump alone are not the masters of generating fake news. The present regime in India is a cut above them in doling out to credulous citizens 'facts' that bear no rational scrutiny. Media is by nature cautious, sceptical and careful in accepting tall claims. Therefore, social media is used for circulating this parallel 'news'. Ideally, social media should have performed its role as a descendant of print and TV media, but as of now, it is being put to use as their adversary.

What should have been respected for its independence as a pillar of democracy is now made to emit trivia flowing out of the regime's propaganda machine. The TV channel news rooms are shrill today because the anchors have lost their own voice. They are busy shouting down dissenting voices rather than raising questions that concern the country and its citizens. The painful loss of nerve by media in India may be a natural consequence of the prevailing political environment. Far more painful is the citizen's complicity. Sadly, a large section of India's citizenry has chosen to remain a mute witness to the silencing of the questioners. In terms of knowledge and economic transactions, media is the producer and citizens are the consumers. However, in order to safeguard our democracy, citizens must see media as a democratic institution and stand by it when it is under attack. If the regime's propaganda pitches media against social media, citizens committed to democracy must attempt to bring the two together in complementary relation.

Most citizens appear to have shifted loyalties away from print and TV media to social media platforms for news and views. They are jubilant that they are no longer mere consumers of media content but also its producers. This excitement and the unmatched speed with which content can be relayed makes social media users impervious to the fact that the terrain is constantly assailed by thought viruses. Besides, the technology which provides social media its user control and speed simultaneously provides the state a vantage ground for mounting an pervasive surveillance, aimed at silencing dissent. This may suit a regime in power for one or two terms, but is disastrous for our democracy and our nation. The situation will not change unless citizens come forward to actively defend the freedom of media and of their minds.

Questions, What?

ON THE FACE OF IT, ASKING A QUESTION APPEARS TO BE A simple act of responding to things with curiosity. Except for what linguists call 'phatic communication' such as 'how are you?' or 'is everything okay?', questions arise in one's mind out of the quest to know. They also arise out of concern for matters that one thinks are important. At a higher pitch, they are born out of philosophical anxiety as in *Hamlet*'s 'To be or not to be?' or the Upanishidic 'Ko aham?' (who am I?). There are times when questions arise out of a collective desire to be assured that all is well with the state. When such questions are asked in the Parliament, the technical term used to describe them is 'interpellation'. When asked outside the Parliament and legislative assemblies by people who are imagined to be silent observers, they reflect the popular perception regarding the functioning of the government. I list here a few questions that people have asked recently, but remained unanswered. When the COVID-19 pandemic broke out, the Prime Minister made an appeal to contribute funds to a new trust called PM CARES created for relief. Citizens wanted to know if the fund was a government entity or a private entity. It continues to remain surrounded by studied ambivalence. During the NDA-1 government, a committee was appointed to review the history of India for the last twelve thousand years, a time span matching with the beginning of the Holocene. Why was no representation given in that committee of experts to anyone from the north-east tribal communities, or from the southern Dravidian communities, or to women? No answer. In view of the India–China border clashes, one would have expected to know if the People's Army of China had crossed into Indian land, and if they had, how deep was the encroachment. There has been no clarity regarding this information. When the international media started talking about snooping by the Pegasus spyware, citizens wanted to know if the government had authorised an Israel-based firm to mount surveillance on private individuals. Again, no answer.

Media reports say that the Sabarmati Ashram is to be renovated and made a world-class tourist destination. On discussing with the trustees of the ashram, the author was told that they have no clear idea of the plans. In the gruesome killings at Lakhimpur in Uttar Pradesh, did the police think of it as a case of murder to be treated under the Indian Penal Code? Why were the suspected killers not arrested immediately? Why were opposition leaders detained without disclosing reasons? These questions were in the minds of not just the citizens of India but even the highest court of India. Yet, no clear answers could be elicited. Recently, two instances of drugs trafficking and consumption shot into news—one involving a few grams of narcotic and the other involving several thousand kilograms. Why the Bombay instance received so much attention as against the Mundra-port instance is a question not likely to be answered. In normal times, the government is expected to answer these questions inside the Parliament as well as outside. However, if the Parliament is made a space where the term 'interpellation' is no longer respected as part of its constitutional duty, it cannot be expected to satisfy the citizens' quest to seek answers. The Parliament session practically ruled out the question hour and opposition benches had to literally struggle to get at least half an hour every day for questions. If elections—that cost the country and its tax payers dearly, and consume a large amount of media time and national attention—do not ultimately result into a means of generating well-informed debates and providing answers, the form of the government that we have today needs to be called by a name other than democracy.

In democratic countries, the media are expected to flag issues of interest, seek answers, form perspectives around them and orient people's response to enable people's representatives to perform well. Barring some courageous individuals and a few honourable media organisations, the electronic and print media in India have clearly moved far away from this age-old media dharma. The symptoms of the abdication of their duty are too well known for me to list them out here. It is the causes of this condition that require our attention. Independent media requires financial independence of media houses. The costs involved are so high that it is no longer possible in our time to even dream, let alone think, of financially self-sufficient media. Gone are the times when print media were ruled by the editorial and opinion desks. For more than half a century, they are being run by media companies or business houses. At this juncture of a fierce war between digits, the social media platforms, and printed characters, the publication and print industry, keeping a print media venture afloat is nothing short of a financial gymnastic miracle. If, on top of the acute financial uncertainty, which was made more acute by the world-wide pandemic, there is the fear of intimidation of media workers and trolling of opinion writers, it is not surprising that media prioritises its own safety. The electronic media ventures are costlier and, for the same reasons, tend to plunge more willingly for their own safety. Though one may not like the idea, the catch-phrase in financial markets is 'media and entertainment industry' (ME), describing a rapidly growing combination of cinema, video games, print entertainment, print and electronic media. There is a rather naive hope that if the constitutional democratic forums and the media can no longer play their traditionally defined roles, social media, at the fingertips of citizens, will salvage democracies from their current aberrations. However, they generate chaotic noise more than well-searched information. Surrounded by so much noise, we live in a no-conversation era, a political arrangement that can probably be called 'no-question regime'.

Restoring Questioning

TWO POEMS WHICH EVERY HIGH-SCHOOL STUDENT IN THE vast British colonial expanse had to study during the nineteenth and early twentieth centuries were 'Daffodils' by William Wordsworth and 'The Village School Master' by Oliver Goldsmith. Wordsworth's lyrical stanzas were all about the excitement in the sudden discovery of the bountiful nature. Goldsmith's couplets evoked a tragicomic nostalgia for the old-world, lost altogether. His schoolmaster was a paradoxical self-proclaimed scholar in the midst of village idiots, an argumentative and adamant intellectual. 'It was certain he could write, and cipher too/Lands he could measure, terms and tides presage/And even the story ran that he could gauge/ In arguing too, the parson owned his skill/For even though vanquished he could argue still.' Since Goldsmith penned 'The Village School Master', every high-school student who read it has found in her own teachers a shadow of the old pastoral England's idiosyncratic teacher. In my mid-twentieth century small-town school, I too had such teachers, full of intellectual views and unwilling to accept any contrary views. One of them was extremely proud of the great glory of the ancient Bharatvarsha. There was another who passionately believed that all that was Western was unquestionably superior. Frequent arguments and predictable disagreement between the two formed a large part of the school's folklore. Subjected to absolute adherence to their own views, I grew up wondering if questioning had any place in schools.

For the last six decades, having studied and taught in Indian schools, colleges and universities, I have noticed that learning and teaching in India are not comfortable with the desire to question. Quite ironically, assessment and grading of students' intellectual assessment is based on their ability to answer a set of 'questions' given in examinations. I have never quite understood how the minds that are not taught to formulate and raise questions can be assessed by asking them to tackle questions in the silence and loneliness of an examination hall. When an entire system of knowledge-transaction is built upon intellectual bankruptcy caused by students' inability to formulate questions, it is not surprising if knowledge institutions too get marooned in intolerance towards questions. Over the decades, I have often been frowned upon by scholars of chemistry for asking 'Why is sea water salty?'—a question not yet conclusively answered—and by Indologists for asking 'If Sanskrit had such a sway on Indian languages in the past, why are most names of fish and birds in India non-Sanskrit?'

It is not as if questioning was not used as a method for developing knowledge in the past. In fact, many of the important Jain, Buddhist and other ancient Indian texts were written in the form of questions and answers. The Bhagwad Gita is a good example. The yaksh-prashnas in the Mahabharata is another. The most illustrious example is a principal Upanishad known as the Prashn Upanishad, or

Prashnopanishad. Composed in the Pippalada line of Vedic textual tradition, it raises questions related to the origin of life. The primary three chapters of its current body of six chapters asked: How were living beings created? Which is the central divine being—*deva*—the spring of life? From where does life come, how does it enter bodies, how does it exit from them, and how does it interact with the 'self' or *chitta*? Those were excellent questions, indeed, and answered in detail in that Upanishad. They point to how similar the initial knowledge transactions in India were to the contemporary Greek knowledge tradition of Socrates and Plato. It must be added, however, that with the deification of the guru and the infantilisation of the shishyas that happened later through India's history, questioning became a casualty. Over the last thousand years, the pan-Indian process of sect formation was, in essence, a process of questioning established dogma and orthodoxy; yet, in their turn, each of the philosophical splinters emerging as sects turned to self-ossification and debarred questioning. Sadly, the ability to raise questions, and more importantly, the ability to examine them and answer them dispassionately, have been systematically suppressed by most social institutions we espouse. Our universities and schools are no exception.

Ever since I entered a university as a lecturer, I have come across instances of institutional reluctance in facing questions. Raising a question—a legitimate question at that—is normally seen as impudence and disobedience. At the Baroda University, where my wife and I used to teach, the ritual of performing Satyanarayan Katha in the university office was introduced when the BJP started ruling Gujarat. When my wife—a scientist—questioned its propriety, the administration decided to block her from becoming the dean of the Faculty of Science. This was by no means a singular instance. In hundreds of universities, many hundreds of academics have faced institutional wrath for raising simple questions. Several universities in the country have also been painted as 'antinational' by media and official agencies when student bodies or professors have raised questions on public policies or national issues.

I received a communication a few days ago from a professor of anthropology at the South Asian University in Delhi. He wrote that four professors—Dr Snehashish Bhattacharya, Dr Srinivas Burra, Dr Irfanullah Farooqi and Dr Ravi Kumar—have been suspended for expressing support to a student protest. The students were protesting against the absence of fair representation in the sexual harassment and gender sensitisation committees and the decrease in student stipend. Instead of resolving the issues, the administration curbed the protest. Just a few days before the faculty suspension in Delhi, Professor Tejswini Desai was punished for discussing the recent communal disturbances in Kolhapur in a class. A few students asked her questions on the issue and she, on her part, helped them understand the complete context of the rising communalism. If such atmosphere in universities and institutions meant for learning continues to prevail, India will have succeeded in annihilating the spirit of enquiry, which ideally should be the heart of education, pivotal in helping humans advance knowledge. But in a regime headed by an individual who disdains questions, can educational institutions have the spine to think differently? The question of questioning needs a serious re-think by all of us in order to bring our democracy back to where it should be. Authoritarian education institutions may be the cheapest software for undemocratic regimes; but they come at a great cost to the future of the nation.

Angry Gods, Angry Mobs

EURIPIDES, LIVING IN THE FIFTH CENTURY BC, UNDERSTOOD that there was much at the heart of tragedy that was comic in essence and much in comedy that was close to tragedy. He demonstrated this in his *Cyclops*, a satyr-play, 'satyr' being a kind of second-class god with horse-ears and tails. One of the characters Euripides created was Polyphemus, a Cyclops, known for his shrill songs, weird stories and fondness for younger men. However, in Greek mythology, Polyphemus was the son of Poseidon, the god of seas. Three centuries before Euripides, Homer had demonstrated Poseidon's violent anger—a consequence of Odysseus making the one-eyed Polyphemus blind. The rage of Poseidon, which makes Odysseus's, voyage home prone to risk, raises some intriguing questions; one, do gods ever get angry; and two, how do mortals know when gods are angry? The answer provided in Greek mythology was that only Hermes, the interpreter, knows when gods are angry. Hermes is the heralder of gods as well as a trickster—somewhat like Narada in Indian mythology. He is also considered the god of travellers, thieves, orators and merchants. The institution of interpreters of gods' moods was not original to Greek mythology. From the thirty-third century BCE, Egyptian dynasts—known as 'pharaoh'—had founded their authority on their ability to interpret god's moods. The Greeks seem to have imbibed the Egyptian idea. A similar echo of 'theological hermeneutics' can be seen in the Indian institution of the vedic purohit, phonetically close to the Egyptian pharaoh (pronounced as 'phe-ro-aa'). Not much is known about the fantasies about god's wrath that the Indus valley inhabitants held. Though their civilisation disintegrated around the nineteenth century BCE, the Harappans have not left behind any archaeological signs that depict their idea of god's anger. Perhaps the Indus civilisation had no interpreters, no orators and no anticipating the Greek Hermes or the vedic purohit. In sharp contrast to the vedic purohit, Buddhism did not have the concept of god's interpreters. The Greek poet Homer was a near contemporary of Gautam Buddha. The Buddha located misery and grief in the minds of human beings, in their inadequate understanding of reality, and not in the whims of gods in another world. Sadly, the purohits managed to oust Buddhism; and soon after, metaphysics rife with superstition came to be seen as 'knowledge'.

The nobler parts of the Vedic and Upanishidic tradition chose to describe anger as a self-destructive emotion. The Gita speaks of it as a cause of delusion, memory loss and destruction. Yet, when interpreters of god's mind assume the form of a coercive social institution, god himself becomes the loser. During the second millennium, the Bhakti movement rebelled against the self-assumed role of purohits as god's interpreters. During the nineteenth century, the resurgence of Hinduism rested on widening access to the divine to all sections of the society. The greatest among our freedom fighters—including

Tagore, Aurobindo and Gandhi—while believing in the idea of god, made humans the centre of spirituality. Dr Ambedkar bravely rebelled against the social domination of purohits and, in works like *Annihilation of Caste* and *Revolution and Counter Revolution,* tried to establish the idea of the superiority of purohits in India's social history as repressive. In Europe, Friedrich Nietzsche could speak of the demise of god; and after Stalin's coercive policies started hurting people, Louise Fischer, Andre Gide, Arthur Koestler and Stephen Spender chose to use the bold phrase 'The God that Failed' as a book title. In the light of this history of gods and their interpreters, it is quite absurd, in the twenty-first century, to be invoking gods to justify the demonstration of anger among humans.

The ethnography of the interpreters of god's anger should be of interest to those of us who believe in the ideas of justice and rule of law upheld by the Constitution. Every year, in a small town called Madhi in the Ahmednagar district of Maharashtra, thousands of people from nomadic communities get together and express their devotion to the deity at the shrine. In recent years, the advocates of purohit-raj have started gradually blocking the devotees' access to the shrine. When asked if this would make their god angry, many of those nomads replied: 'No, our god is not angry, we are angry.' They were honest and had not surrendered their ability to think. Around four decades ago, I used to teach at the M.S. University of Baroda. There was a small temple inside the campus. When communal riots broke out in the 1990s, one of my colleagues remarked that if the faculty did not side with the majority community, the god on the campus would feel betrayed and angry. This reminded me of a poem by Sri Aurobindo. Eight decades before my time, he used to teach on the same campus. Explaining a sudden and unjustified burst of anger, he wrote, apologetically, 'It was not me, but my belly's hungry god that was angry.' There is no doubt that it is humans who get angry when there are no jobs, when prices continue to go up or when bulldozers destroy their houses. In an attempt to divert people's attention from the hunger in the belly—the actual source of anger—clever interpreters invent trivial gestures and incidents that would insult the gods. Credulous mobs take the cue and attack the misconstrued expression in the work of painters, artists, singers, writers, cartoonists, protesters, critics, opponents and minorities—all in the name of god. Hermes wins, the journey home for Odysseus gets longer and Buddha is forced to remain in exile. If we continue to be led by the interpreters of god's moods, we may as well find ourselves sliding back to the era when science had not yet replaced myth. The era described by historians as the Dark Ages.

Death by Wish

MOHAN DELKAR, A MEMBER OF PARLIAMENT (MP), WAS not a widely known politician. However, in Dadra and Nagar Haveli, a tiny union territory, and in the tribal districts in South Gujarat, he was seen as quite a phenomenon. He was elected as an MP several times and had a sway over most assembly constituencies in the southern tribal talukas of Gujarat. One day, he was found dead in a hotel in Mumbai. A suicide note left behind by him points to victimisation and harassment by official agencies as the reason behind his decision. His note was not as elaborate as the sixty-page note left by Kalikho Pul, a one-time CM of Arunachal Pradesh, who ended his life in August 2016. He had placed on record under the title 'Mere Vichar' (My Thoughts)—an elaborate account of his rise in politics and the rot he saw around him. It gave details of how even Supreme Court judges carried a price tag and how judgments could be influenced. An indictment of the system made by individuals who can no longer be summoned to provide further testimony and witness carries an inherent limitation as a source of factual record. However, they need to be read not as fact-sheets, but as pointers to a harsh truth. In 2016, another suicide note was left behind by Rohith Vemula, a young student in Hyderabad. It said that he wanted to be a writer, but there was a big gap between his mind and body. His body, Vemula felt, was a fatal accident. He wrote, 'The value of a man was reduced to his immediate identity and nearest possibility. To a vote! To a number! To a thing! Never was a man treated as a mind.' Rohit Vemula's note lays bare the social malaise arising out of caste identity. So does the suicide note of Dr Payal Tadvi, a tribal woman who trained as a gynaecologist and worked at the Nair Hospital in Mumbai. Realising that her social identity as an Adivasi was coming in her way as a medical professional, she decided to end her life barely a year after she started her medical practice. The notes left by Kalikho Pul and Mohan Delkar, on the other hand, express their utter dismay with politics in India.

Do these tragic shockers have a message for us as a country? Nearly six decades ago, historian Upendra Thakur published a study under the title *The History of Suicide in India* (1963). He observed that the actual number of suicides in India is much higher than the cases reported in official data. The National Crime Records Bureau of India (NCRB), which keeps the record, reported 1,35,445 deaths by suicides in 2012. The NCRB data, read in the light of Upendra Thakur's well researched observation, indicates that suicide cases have an alarming scale. The World Health Organization (WHO) too maintains suicide statistics. The latest WHO data places India 16th on the 'suicide profusion scale' among the 194 countries covered by it. The global average is 10.6 points (suicides per 1,00,000 persons). Suicide incidence in India is 16, which is one and a half times the global average. The situation is quite alarming, though the seriousness tends to get neglected by conflating farmers' suicides driven by their indebtedness with a rejection of the world—an even more disturbing sign of our time. It has been quite a while since India has left its farmers to die a slow death. The present regime's complete indifference to them is its climax. However, suicidal tendency and incidence of suicide prevail in other sections of society as well. Guru Dutt, Silk Smitha, Nafisa Joseph, Kuljeet Randhwa, Kunal Singh, Jiah Khan and Sushant Singh Rajput were celebrities, not nameless farmers. The truth is that the suicidal tendency in the Indian population cannot be understood if it is seen merely in terms of numbers. If numbers alone is truth, the deaths by COVID-19, may have exceeded deaths by suicide for the peak period of the pandemic. However, while the pandemic surely deserved national attention, so does the growing rate of suicides in the country.

The question here is not about death and its medical and anatomical aspects. It is also not about the criminal nature accorded to committing or abetting suicide. The question that these alarmingly large number of suicides make one ask is: Is there something fundamentally wrong with India, driving some of us to reject the order of things? I was recently going through the Dictionary of Martyrs (1857–1947) prepared by the Indian Council of Historical Research. Its volume for the erstwhile Bombay state lists nearly 1,500 names of individuals who died, in most cases knowing that they would die, in the name of freedom for India. These include persons from all castes, communities and cultural backgrounds. Many of them were the second- or third-generation ancestors of the farmers who committed suicide in recent times. The martyrs' acceptance of death, painful and tragic as it had been for them and their families, had no shade of rejection of the human order. It was, if one may imagine on their behalf, an affirmation of hope for a glorious, free future. However, today's suicides tell a different story. The suicides of India's farmers, artists, social activists, medical professionals, IIT students, housewives and politicians are an indication that the rot is not just limited to economic inequality, caste discrimination, oppression of women and hopelessly bankrupt knowledge systems. It is much deeper than that. It was India that produced thousands of young men and women who willingly sacrificed their lives during the freedom struggle. Suicide is not mere death. It is death invited as an escape. Guru Dutt's outcry in his classic of despair *Pyasa*, *'Jala do, jala do, jala do yeh duniya'* — 'hell with your degenerate world' — accurately captures that sentiment. Suicide, apart from all other things it means, is a declaration of degeneration of things. The rampant incidence of suicide is a telling comment on how we have abetted the degeneration of every system, every source of hope — from the Constitution to courts, from school to sachivalaya, from ideal to idiom. We may be a GDP-fat country, but are we doing well on the happiness index? No, clearly not. Perhaps it is time to envision a new India once again.

People in Ward Number Six

Anton Chekhov's *Ward Number Six* (1892) has Andrey Yefimitch Ragin, a doctor in a small town, as its main character. His quest for philosophical conversation brings him closer to one of the five patients in the lunatic ward, a man clear of reason and forceful in logical arguments. The intimacy between them becomes the reason why the authorities push Dr Ragin into the ward as a madman, making it a ward of six. Manto's 1955 story 'Toba Tek Singh' revolves around the transfer of inmates from an asylum in Lahore to India following Partition. Bishen Singh, from the town Toba Tek Singh, the central character, much like Chekov's doctor, is the only sane person in the midst of the madness generated by the tumultuous events of 1947. He refuses to belong either to Pakistan or to India. For systems that dictate what truth is, such persons have always been a nuisance. As I write this column, my thoughts go back to Chekov and Manto. I do not have the large creative vision they had; yet, I find it necessary to engage in an imaginary conversation with them. The other conversations in this 'rational' world have already turned absurd. Here is an example.

I have been closely watching the progressive unfolding of the social engineering being carried out by the current regime in India. Beginning with the Citizenship Amendment Act, moving through the economic boycott of Muslims in Karnataka, wrecking of the hijab issue, various state regulations related to inter-faith marriages, curb on UGC fellowships for students belonging to scheduled castes, providing funds for genetic studies focused on 'purity' and tweaking of the OBC quota, it has now come to launching a population control policy. When possible, I write on these issues, to remind fellow countrymen that India has a Constitution and we need to adhere to it. I normally try to educate myself on any issue that I want to write about.

Therefore, when I wanted to comment on the proposed Population Control Bill, pending in the Parliament, I checked the sources for exact details. On 26 November 2022, the internet showed a bill introduced by a Rajasthan-based BJP MP as being listed, and the draft of the bill was available for one to read. There was another bill which had been proposed previously and supported by 125 MPs, but it was withdrawn. There were also media reports on a third bill in the pipeline that another BJP MP would propose. The one that was available on the internet to read had all the usual incentives and disincentives associated with any 'stringent population control legislation'. But it had another shocking element in it. It had proposed 'disenfranchisement' of the offenders, the people who have more than two children. To take away the voting rights of citizens under any circumstances is entirely against citizens' rights granted by the Constitution. I wrote my piece and sent it to the editor as I normally do, some two weeks before it was to appear in print. However, closer to the date of its publication, I received a call from the editorial section informing me that they could not locate the document on which I had commented. I was travelling when I got the call. And so, I assured them that once I got back to my desk, I would send it to them. However, when I opened my computer to look for it, I was in for a shock. It no longer existed. All references to it on the internet had disappeared. This had never happened before. I spent a considerable amount of time trying to dig up traces of the document. But it had been meticulously cleaned. This sent a shudder down my spine. Had I fantasised the existence of the bill? Had a deep insanity set in, leading me to imagine an entire parliamentary document when it did not exist? To ward off the thought, I decided to check all my downloads from the date I had written the piece. And, the Google record showed, minute by minute, all my web-related activity. It listed all the sites I had visited before writing the article. But, as I attempted to open one site after another, I noticed that all the matter that I had accessed from the government's official websites had been removed. The other sites I had visited continued to exist in the form I had seen them. I would have closed the matter there; but I remembered that sometime back, the census sites which I had referred to in the past too were made inaccessible. Besides, in place of the proposed bill, a new announcement, by the very BJP MP who was to propose a population control bill, started appearing in media. A few TV channels organised discussions around the new bill. I could not access its exact text, but media reports still have comments on it.

What is this phenomenon? Is it a way of assessing public opinion on the question of population? Is it just an indication of the indecisiveness of the party in power on the issue? Or is it an exercise in political messaging? If giving glimpses of such documents to the public, and then withdrawing them from the public view is being attempted as political messaging, the implied message is to stereotype minorities without any respect for facts and figures related to birth rates, population statistics, infant mortality rates and infertility levels. Besides, the frequent disappearance of data from public view amounts to a complete mockery of the citizen's right to information. Allowing shocking ideas to be first circulated and then mopping them up to give the impression that they were never stated is an old hand-trick in the mass psychology of fascism. Are we already there? Has India become another ward number six?

Disenfranchising the Poor

IN A DEMOCRACY, PEOPLE MATTER ABOVE EVERYTHING ELSE. When people are looked at with scorn, it is a sure sign of the weakening of democracy. The description of democracy—'by, for and of the people'—originating in John Wycliffe's 1384 prologue to his Bible translation, and later echoed in the US in 1858 by Theodore Parker and endorsed by Abraham Lincoln, is known to every child throughout the world. People's representatives, therefore, are expected to respect people on whose historical consent the parliament is founded. However, in practice, this norm is violated more than it is observed. Yet, when the parliament itself is used for stereotyping a particular section of the population, the foundations of democracy get corroded beyond measure. The often-expressed desire of the BJP to create a population control policy is one such act, ostensibly benign but profoundly anti-people. During the last few years, various BJP leaders have articulated the need to bring in a stringent legislation for population control. Among the recent ones is the proposed Bill No. 45 of 2022 by Chandra Prakash Joshi, BJP MP from Chittorgarh.

The pending bill proposes a watchdog committee to monitor population, based on the populist assumption that since the population of India is likely to exceed the population of China in the near future (which it now already has), it is necessary to 'control' it now. It states as its rationale—'China has been successful in controlling its population by making laws and implementing them strictly. There is also a need for a similar population control law in India so that the population can be controlled.' The method proposed in the bill is a far too simplistic combination of incentives and disincentives. It proposes that couples with two or less living children shall be entitled to a) free treatment in primary health centres (PHCs); b) priority in promotion and c) scholarship for higher education for their children. In contrast, if a couple has more than two living children, neither the husband nor the wife shall be entitled to a) contest elections to government bodies; b) exercise the right to vote; c) benefits of government schemes; d) government jobs; e) benefits of government scholarships and f) be employed in a government institution. The proposed provisions are in violation of individual liberties. Besides, preventing any person from exercising their franchise violates the Indian Constitution. Universal franchise is the most precious right that the Constitution has granted to its citizens; and unless pertaining to a rare case of criminality, the state has the responsibility to protect this right.

The assumptions on which the proposed bill is based too are questionable. It is true that the population of India is increasing and it has now exceeded the Chinese population, which was restricted through a population policy of disincentives. However, the negative consequences of the policy in China have left the Chinese government seriously worried. The 'one child policy' of China has already led to severe female infanticide and gender imbalance, with the current male population exceeding the female population by nearly 30 million. In the last four decades since the policy was introduced in 1979, the aged population has increased dramatically, while the proportion of the young and working population has alarmingly reduced. The policy was aimed at peaking at 1.4 billion—which it did—and then reducing the population by half by 2100. However, China has now realised that the enormous shortage of working-age population, and a further shortage of females among them, will soon translate into an economic crisis with global ramifications. Therefore, no country in the world would like to emulate the Chinese population policy. A disproportionately high ageing population is a cause of worry not just in China, but also for several other countries like Japan in Asia, Brazil in South America and Italy in Europe. Several studies predict a severe lowering of the GDP for these countries as they are expected to struggle to gain a 'population dividend'. Among demographers, it is common wisdom that a fertility rate of just over 2 is the 'stabilising' rate for any population, particularly the populations that do not have adequate and accessible healthcare systems in place.

India, placed number 96 in global ranking with a fertility rate of 2.1, has the benefit of having an adequate proportion of young and working population and no great risks of increased fertility in the foreseeable future. What is most remarkable is that India reached 2.1, coming down from 5.9 in 1950, 5.7 in 1960, 4.9 in 1970, 4.2 in 1980, 3.4 in 1990 and 2.8 in 2000. This was achieved not through any stringent population law but through gender empowerment, active promotion of contraception use and educating all irrespective of religion and gender. It may be interesting to compare the decade-by-decade fall in fertility rates in India with the global average (GAFR). When the GAFR was 5 in 1960, India was at 5.9. In 1980, GAFR was 3.8 and India was at 4.9. Cut to 2010, this huge gap was reduced, with GAFR at 2.57 and the Indian FR at 2.8. These figures clearly indicate that maintaining population levels does not require punitive population policies. What it requires is empowerment of women and universal access to education.

A government obsessed with rapid privatisation of education and healthcare is a greater risk to Indian population than its fertility rate. The risk is directly proportionate to infant mortality rates. If poor people know that their offsprings do not have much chance of survival, they will naturally desire to produce more children for their own welfare. In 2022, our IMR was 27.695 (deaths per 1,000 births). It was 30.924 in 2019, 29.848 in 2020 and 28.771 in 2021. The mix up with the figures of COVID-19 deaths needs a separate study. In addition to infant mortality, we also face a greater impact of climate change. Climate historian Gwen Robbins Schug has warned that human populations in semi-arid regions of the world, including South Asia, currently face disproportionate impacts from global climate change. Schug points to how climate change had resulted in a reduced population around four millennia before our time. Considering all these facts, our present fertility rate of 2.1 calls for no drastic reduction.

The BJP and the RSS propaganda about the Muslim population soon overtaking the Hindu population in India is as ridiculous as their claim that Muslims and Catholic Christians produce more children. The statistics of populations in various countries—Christian, Muslim and Buddhist—shows that poverty and lack of education and healthcare are the reasons for excessive population growth. Theologies do not have any direct relation to the human desire to regenerate and maintain populations. The impending bill in the Parliament has no justification, either in fact or in economic or sociological wisdom. Should the brute majority of the BJP in the Parliament turn it into law, it will result in the division of an already divided society. Worst still, by disenfranchising a large number of poor in the country, it will bring India one step closer to the idea of a Hindu-brahminical raj fantasised in the *Manusmriti*.

A Hindi India

About two thousand years ago, Tholkappiyar, the fabled author of *Tolkappiyam*, said that poetic words can be distributed in four types: Lyarcol, Thirisol, Thisaiccol and Vadasol. Of these, he held, 'Vadasol'—words from northern languages—'become fit to be used in Tamil only when they adopt Tamil phonetics discarding their northern phonetics'.

From ancient times, sensitivity to language difference has almost formed the core of Dravidic selfhood. A similar sensitivity existed among the speakers of Prakrits in ancient times. It was in one of the Prakrits that Mahavir had presented his teachings in the sixth century BCE. Eighteen centuries later, Acharya Hemachandra, a major Jain scholar, poet, mathematician and philosopher, produced his *Desinamamala*, a treatise on the importance of Prakrit words used in Gujarat during his time, as against those from Sanskrit. In the process, he gave a tangible form to the Gujarati language. Mahatma Gandhi, who defined the idea of selfhood for India in *Hind Swaraj* (1909), chose to write this iconic book in Gujarati. As such, language sensitivity has been a feature of selfhood in the case of every Indian language.

It would be unreasonable to expect a contemporary Indian to know about a two-thousand-year-old *Tolkappiyam* or a nine-century-old *Desinamamala*. But would it be too much to expect the person to know about the Constitution adopted by the republic seven decades ago? The Constitution states two things with utmost clarity. One, India is 'a union of states'; and two, the official language used for communication between the states shall be the language that had been in use at the time of adoption of the Constitution. The move from English to Hindi can take place only if, as articles related to languages unambiguously state, 'two or more states agree' for the shift. Article 344 (4) provides for a committee consisting of thirty members, twenty from the Parliament and ten from the state assemblies, for safeguarding language-related provisions.

The functions and the scope of the committee, as laid down by the Constitution, are further clarified by the practice of sharing 'language' as a subject between two ministries, the Ministry of Human Resource Development (MHRD) and the Ministry of Home Affairs. The scope of the MHRD with reference to language extends to education and the promotion of cultural expression. On the other hand, the scope of the Ministry of Home Affairs extends to safeguarding relations of the states with the 'union', protecting the linguistic rights of language minorities and the promotion of Hindi. The last of these, the Constitution states, has to be 'without interference with other languages'.

In light of the provisions in the Constitution, two crucial questions need to be addressed to the Ministry of Home Affairs and its Hindi Language Committee: Has Hindi seen any growth during the last seven decades? If yes, does it interfere with the growth of other scheduled languages?

Data from the census tell quite a story. In 2011, Hindi speakers accounted for 43.63 per cent of the total population, with a total of 52.83 crore speakers. In 1971, the number was 20.27 crore, accounting for 36.99 per cent of the total population. Between 2001 and 2011, the growth in proportion of the population was 2.6 per cent. The next most spoken language, Bangla (the first is Hindi) had negative growth. It was spoken by 8.30 per cent of Indians in 1991, 8.11 per cent in 2001 and 8.03 per cent in 2011. Telugu, which slid from 7.87 per cent in 1991 to 7.19 per cent in 2001 and 6.70 per cent in 2011, has a similar story to tell.

The Odiya language too experienced negative growth—1981-91-3.35 per cent; 1991-2001-3.21 per cent and 2001-2011-3.10 per cent. It is no different for Marathi either: 7.45 per cent of India's population (1991), 6.99 per cent (2001) and 6.86 per cent (2011). Tamil, the oldest surviving language in the country, should have received at least some attention from the Ministry of Home Affairs. But its case is no different from that of Bangla, Telugu and Marathi. Tamil speakers accounted for 6.32 per cent of the total population in 1991, but went down to 5.91 per cent in 2001 and 5.70 per cent in 2011. The only major language to show decadal growth (though small) was Gujarati. And the only small yet scheduled language to show good growth was Sanskrit. The 2021 Census, when conducted, will carry out another count of languages in the country. And for reasons that are too obvious, the situation of all languages in the Eighth Schedule—except Hindi and Sanskrit, and perhaps Gujarati—will have worsened. In this context, the parliamentary committee for the promotion of Hindi should have expressed its concern about the decline of Indian languages, except Hindi, and the growth of Sanskrit, which has ceased to be a living language since the ninth century.

If all other languages show a relative decline, why is Hindi recording steady growth? This is because the 52.83 crore speakers of Hindi (as recorded in 2011) included not just the speakers of 'Hindi' but also those of more than 50 other languages. Bhojpuri, which was claimed by more than five crore speakers, and evident in the growing visibility gained by its cinema, literature, newspapers, songs, theatre and publication industry, is categorised as Hindi. Most languages of Himachal Pradesh, Uttarakhand, Chhattisgarh, Rajasthan and Jharkhand have also been pushed within the category of Hindi. Even the Pawari language (spoken mainly in Maharashtra and in some parts of Madhya Pradesh) is classified as 'Hindi', overlooking the fact that most Pawari speakers may find Hindi almost unintelligible.

Thus, the story of Hindi's growth is quite fictitious. Had the census not included these other languages under Hindi, the strength of Hindi speakers would have gone down to about 39 crores—just a little under 32 per cent of the total population in 2011—and would have looked not too different from those of other scheduled languages. The committee should have concerned itself with making the census data for Hindi more realistic. The data for English speakers appears to have been trimmed. Census 2011 reports a total of 3,88,793 Indians as English speakers (2,59,678 men and 1,29,115 women). Compare this with the least spoken among the scheduled languages, that is, Manipuri at 17.61 lakh speakers and Bodo at 14.82 lakh speakers. No further comment is necessary to show how there is nothing to be proud about these figures.

Hindi is a beautiful language, as is the case with any language in the world. Hindi cinema has brought India fame and foreign currency. Hindi literature is rich and evokes pride when mentioned. Yet, it is also true that among the languages included in the Eighth Schedule, it falls within the younger lot of languages. On the other hand, Tamil, Kannada, Kashmiri, Marathi, Oriya, Sindhi, Nepali and Assamiya have a much older history. As languages of knowledge too, Tamil, Kannada, Bangla and Marathi (with their abundance of encyclopaedias and historical literature) quite easily outshine Hindi. A language evolves slowly; it cannot be forced to grow by issuing ordinances.

If knowledge related to the history of Hindi, India's multilingualism, the federal structure of India and the issue of language sensitivity in so many states guided the Official Language Committee to accept linguistic realism, what is it that prompted Home Minister Amit Shah to call for a Hindi India all of a sudden? It is perhaps not so much the ideology of the RSS of hyphenating Hindi-Hindu nationalism that has prompted the Home Minister's Hindi assertion. It may also not be the BJP's idea of majoritarian democracy that has prompted it. Hindi speakers in the country, despite the inflated figure of 52 crore against 121 crore put out by the 2011 Census, do not form a linguistic majority. The fact remains that 69 crore (even in the 2011 Census) were non-Hindi speakers. In that sense, it is not—and cannot be—the majority language of India. It is quite likely that Mr Shah's attempt to stoke Hindi pride is a balm to ease the pain of the vast unemployment that hurts the youth in the Hindi belt, an area so crucial for the BJP's electoral performance. Yet, the Home Minister has overlooked the fact that while harping on Pakistan as a threat to security works for Hindu mobilisation, depicting English as an anti-national entity will no longer work to mobilise the Hindi-speaking people. It makes for utterly poor economics and absurd linguistics. Most of all, it makes for anti-federal politics. Does India really need these?

Language Mix and Paranoia

THE HISTORY OF THE ENGLISH WORD 'TEXT' IS INTRICATELY woven together with the history of the word 'textile'. They both originate in early Latin, with 'text' meaning 'weave'. Every word has its unmistakable texture. It can only be stretched so much. Stretching it beyond its limit makes the word either inoperative or plainly ridiculous. For instance, the Hindi coinage 'notebandi' is adequate to describe 'demonitisation'. In music, another field where 'notes' and 'notation' are of key significance, using 'notebandi' to mean dropping of certain notes may result in an unintended paradox, for 'bandh' also refers to the format of a composition. The term 'jashan', like every other word in any language, has a rich fabric of its own. Metaphorically speaking, it is woven in ancient times by bringing together threads from the Indo-Aryan, Indo-Iranian and Indo-European. 'Jashan' is not just the phonetically similar 'joyous' of English but also semantically almost identical, for they have a shared historical texture. Several other words in English beginning with the letter 'j' have shades of meaning that 'jashan' expresses. Take, for instance, the loud conversation in 'jabber', the bold colours of lace in 'jabot', the social intimacy in 'joviality', the merrymaking in 'jamboree', the lively dance in 'jig' or *'joie de vivre'* drawn by English from French. The linguistic fabric that made 'jasn' or 'yasn' in Sanskrit or its Hindi derivative 'jasan' also made many words in old Persian, Latin and many modern European languages mean joy. In different cultures and different times, they got wedded to different grammars and different rules of morphology, at times turning 'j' into 'y', 's' into 'sh' and so on.

Recently, the fabric of the joy word came for a new twist, resulting in terrifying anger. The case was, as school grammar will tell us, the possessive case with the use of the conjunctive 'of'. 'Jashn' was joined by 'e', the Persian case marker, to an Urdu word. The current fashion in political discourse is to describe it as 'mlenchha' (polluting), threatening the social fabric of India. In languages, every word-compounding—*sandhi*—is either a cross-border union or an intra-language love affair. If compound words do not bring about the ghar-wapasi of meaning, they get to be seen as love jihad. The Bhagavad Gita describes anger as the beginning of derangement: *'krodhat bhavati sammoha, sammohat smruti-vibhramah'* (anger breeds delusion, delusion corrupts memory). In tune with this observation, it was forgotten that the word 'wapasi' is from another language. The bitter truth is that 'jalebis', 'halwa' and even 'barfi', relished during Diwali, are sired by Arabic ancestors. Are we being bulldozed towards considering language purity as a part of our national identity? If that is the case, one fears that our more than seventy-five year old 'aazadi' will not be seen as pure freedom unless you call it swatantrata; and the shaheeds—martyrs—who sacrificed their lives will not be seen as patriotic enough unless you call them 'shouryadhar'. The day is not far when we will be asked to call

Subhas Chandra Bose's Azad Hind Sena the Swatantra Bharat Sena. The new India cannot tolerate a term whose root is in the Proto-Iranian *azata*—free—though many words in the Rig Veda itself come from the Avestan.

Since its inception, the RSS has been excessively fond of using words drawn from Sanskrit. Given that its makers were drawn from brahminical circles in Maharashtra obsessed with language purity, this was somewhat natural. Besides, it had swallowed the view of India's past proposed by William Jones and other Indologists lock, stock and barrel—India prior to the eleventh century was all glory before succumbing to a steady decline. Naturally, such a view saw all that was in Sanskrit as flawless knowledge, and all that came in the post-Sanskrit era as a degradation of India's 'pure' heritage. Having once accepted this simplistic view of the past, the RSS has never once revisited or questioned it. However, the instances of attacks on language-mixing during the NDA era go much beyond a simplistic devotion to the Sanskrit language.

One of the advanced branches of language study is used to detect mental health disorders. Seen from that perspective, the hyper-sensitive response of the Hindutva lumpen to terms originating in Arabic, Turkish, Kurdish, Urdu and Pakhto indicate a worrisome trend. The technical term used by psychology for it is paranoia. It refers to a person or a group that is given to doubting the loyalty and trustworthiness of others, is reluctant to confide information in others fearing that they are against them, holds grudges, reads hidden meaning in otherwise innocent words, is constantly assailed by moods of suspicion without reason, is hostile, stubborn and argumentative, and tends to develop negative stereotypes of those from another cultural context. In this illness, the imaginary fear of persecution aggravates hostile response as a cover for unwillingness to undertake situation analysis and problem solving. When the entire business world is worried about the economic decline induced by the loss of social harmony, when minorities and marginalised communities are gripped by a sense of insecurity and threat, when unemployment and food insecurity are mounting, the overstated language sensitivity and the hostile response to it indicate the pathology of a disorder. This is not just one of many Hindutva idiosyncrasies; it is a lot more worrisome trend. The quizzical tag-lines in certain brand advertisements and virulent attacks on them may appear merely as bizarre interludes to most of us, deserving no serious attention. However, if the regime slides into paranoia, without willingness to do situation analysis and making attempts at solving real problems, it will affect the lives of millions. If it continues to think that communal amity can be disrupted for gains in every state election, the loss to the country, its people, its economy and its future can far outweigh the petty electoral gains for a single party, whether it wants to speak of 'joy' in Sanskrit, Urdu, Tamil or any other language under the sun.

A Return to the Returning of Awards

Dr M.M. Kalburgi was assassinated at his residence in Dharwad on 30 August 2015. The murder shocked the country and triggered a country-wide intellectual protest. It was a protest against the growing intolerance in the country. The supporters of the government mistook it as an anti-government protest. It was variously dubbed as a 'manufactured protest', 'move to spread disaffection towards the state', 'Congress-induced protest' and 'insult to the nation'. No representative from the authorities made any attempt to understand from the writers, dramatists and film-makers what prompted them to return the awards they earned for their high-talent and creativity.

In February 2017, a question was asked in the Lok Sabha by BJP's Om Birla to find out how many writers had returned their awards since 2015 and if they had accepted the 'government's request to take back the awards'. The Minister of Culture at the time was Mahesh Sharma. Sumitra Mahajan was the Lok

Sabha Speaker. The minister's reply included a list of writers: (Hindi)—Uday Prakash, Ashok Vajpeyi, Krishna Sobti, Mangalesh Dabral, Kashinath Singh, Rajesh Joshi; (English)—G.N. Devy, Nayantara Sahgal, Keki Daruwalla; (Gujarati)—Anil Joshi; (Punjabi)—Waryam Singh Sandhu, Surjit Patar, Jaswinder, Gurbachan Bhullar, Atamjit Singh, Baldev Singh, Darshan Butter, Ajmer Singh Aulakh, Mohan Bhandari; (Rajasthani)—Nand Bhardwaj, Ambika Dutt; (Kannada)—Kum Veerbhadrappa, Rahamat Tarikere, Devanuru Mahadeva; (Kashmiri)—Ghulam Nabi Khayal, Margoob Banihali; (Urdu)—Munawwar Rana, Khaleel Mamoon; (Malayalam)—Sara Joseph; (Assamese)—Homen Borgohain, Nirupama Borgohain; (Telugu)—Katyayani Vidmahe; Translation Prize–(Hindi)—Chaman Lal; (Kannada)—G.N. Ranganatha Rao; (Marathi)—Ibrahim Afgan; Yuva Puraskar—(English)—Aman Sethi; (Punjabi)—Pragat Singh Satauj; and the Bal Sahitya Purskar—(Telugu)—M. Bhoopal Reddy.

The minister stated: 'Yes, Madam … The writers claimed that there was an attack on their freedom of expression and the Akademi kept silent on the issue … The Akademi had convened a special Executive Board meeting on 23 October 2015 and 17 December 2015 in which a resolution had been passed requesting the writers to reconsider their decision.' He did not mention that the Sahitya Akademi Awards are not government awards, but rather, they are awarded by an autonomous body of writers, entirely run by writers. Nor did he elaborate on what 'the issue' was on which the Sahitya Akademi had maintained silence as claimed by the writers who had returned the awards. Unsurprisingly, the murders of Dr Narendra Dabholkar, Comrade Govind Pansare and Dr M.M. Kalburgi were not mentioned by the minister in his response. Six months later, Gauri Lankesh was assassinated in Bangalore

(5 September 2017). As before, many TV channels ridiculed the writers as persons who had expressed their 'disavowal and disaffection towards the state', a phrase that the age-old sedition law had coined.

Almost a century ago, in protest of the Jallianwala Bagh massacre, India's greatest modern writer, Rabindranath Tagore, had returned the King George Honour given to him for his contribution to literature, which had made him 'Sir Rabindranath'. In his letter to the Viceroy, he had stated: 'The time has come when badges of honour make our shame glaring in their incongruous context of humiliation, and I for my part wish to stand, shorn of all special distinctions, by the side of those of my countrymen, who, for their so-called insignificance, are liable to suffer a degradation not fit for a human beings.' This act, carried out during the British rule, was not seen then as an act of sedition.

Several BJP leaders mocked the returning of awards as a 'manufactured protest', a phrase brought into currency by the late Arun Jaitley. Writers tried to repeatedly state that there was no 'hidden manufacturer' to their protest. The poet Keki N. Daruwalla made it a point to stress in his letter to the President of Sahitya Akademi: 'I wish to make it clear that I have no party leanings ... the landscape that confronts the writer today is bleak ... Faces will continue to be blackened with paint and painters like M.F. Husain will be forced into exile. A writer like Taslima Nasreen will have to leave Kolkata under a leftist regime. Statesmen will continue to be praised for their nationalism *despite* the fact they are Muslims. Mob murders will continue to be described as accidents.'

A similar strain ran through all the statements issued by writers who had returned their honours. The question of political affiliation was immaterial in this unique phenomenon.

What mattered was their emphasis on the increased intolerance in social life. In my statement sent to the Sahitya Akademi I had said, 'Writers and thinkers have come forward to rescue sense, good-will, values, tolerance and mutual respect ... The great idea of India is based on a profound tolerance for diversity and difference. They far surpass everything else in importance.'

In 1964, Jean Paul Sartre declined to accept the Nobel Prize for Literature given to him. None of the official records of the Swedish Academy or the French government have ever censured Sartre. They understand that writers and artists function as the conscience of the people and display the courage to challenge the state. The Parliamentary Committee Report recently tabled in the Parliament shows the utter failure of the current regime in understanding the autonomy of the artist's conscience. We have reason to feel glad that at least one member of the committee recorded dissent. If the recommendations made by the committee get implemented in the future, India should never hope to see another Tagore. If subservience to the state takes precedence over the call of conscience, the idea of democracy and freedom of thought will have no chance of existence.

The Return of the Mahabharata

'THE FARMERS ARE CAMPING ALONG FIVE MAJOR HIGHWAYS on the outskirts of New Delhi and have said they won't leave until the government rolls back what they call the "black laws".' This was the news on the 8 December 2020, the day on which the nation observed a voluntary lockdown, a Bharat Bandh. A group of farmers in Karnataka I met on the day of the bandh commented that these five camps are like the five Pandavas. The unexpected analogy set me thinking. Thousands of farmers had set out on an unprecedented march from Punjab, the land of five rivers. Their destination was New Delhi, which in ancient times was Indraprastha. Twelve days earlier, on 27 November, they were stopped by the Haryana Police who dug trenches on their way, used water cannons and raised massive barricades. The site of the clash was not too far from the ancient Kurukshetra where the Mahabharata war is believed to have taken place. The time of the year too was the month of Margashirsha, intimately associated with the plot of the ancient war. From the moment the farmers arrayed themselves for the confrontation, the media gaze—the

Divya Chakshu—turned to the epicentre of the action. In the Mahabharata, Sanjay, gifted with divine vision, was charged with the task of presenting a blow-by-blow account of the war to the blind father of the Kauravas.

The initial day on the ancient Kurukshetra war was spent shouting war-slogans and blowing insignia-conches. Until the tenth day, Bhishma was the general on the Kaurava side. Bhishma was shot through, but he waited for his death till the end of Margashirsha. Drona, who followed Bhishma as the general, lasted for five days, followed by Karna who lasted for three days and finally followed by Shalya who presided over the defeat of the Kaurava army. Coming to the farmers' protest, minister Narendra Singh Tomar was fielding for the government in the initial ten days of the agitation. Tomar was eventually sidelined and the action moved into minister Amit Shah's residence on the eleventh day. Besides, in the background, there is the construction of the Central Vista and its foundation-laying ceremony—permitted by the Supreme Court—starkly reminiscent of the palace building in the epic. Presenting yet another contrast were the million lamps lit up at the ghats of Ganga to mark Diwali, even as the 'love-jihad' law by the UP government emboldened vigilante groups to swoop down on Hindu girls in love with Muslim boys, no less demeaning than the undraping of Draupadi in the ancient epic. Though superficial, the similarities between the current political situation in India and the Mahabharata are eye-catching. The ancient epic depicts a war for the protection of 'racial purity'. 'Kulkshaya', the loss of the pure lineage and 'pollution of women by others' were among the main reasons presented by Arjuna to Krishna, explaining his reluctance to go to war, as stated in the beginning of the Bhagawad Gita. Krishna's advice was to stay steadfast in one's duty, the dharma, as the Gita described it. The Gita marked the first day of the epic war. 26 November celebrated as, Constitution Day in India, marked the beginning of the farmers' march. Indeed, the scale of the confrontation between the farmers and the government was epic. The Mahabharata was set in times that witnessed the historic transition of society from pastoralism to agriculture. The current confrontation is set during the time when society is witnessing a shift from responsible democratic state to a form of crony capitalism displayed by an authoritarian government. All that the Pandavas demanded was their right over Hastinapur. All that the farmers demand is the repeal of the recent farm laws. Their argument is that if the government does not provide the minimum support price for their produce, they would be rendered vulnerable to the vagaries of the open market. Those among our countrymen who are not directly engaged in agriculture as a profession tend to think that if other sectors such as banking, insurance, healthcare and education have already been handed over to private players, why not agriculture? Every day, economists have been asking this question in TV debates. While the logic in this question is flawless, the understanding of the issue is deeply flawed. The agrarian society is not just a 'sector'; it is a distinct civilisation, particularly in the case of India, Iran and Egypt. These are countries which, in ancient times, gave birth to distinct civilisations influenced by a shift from pastoralism to agriculture. Indian farmers are, if described from a comprehensive historical perspective, the true makers of India. The nation did not create Indian farmers; the farmers created the Indian nation. Farming is not just an occupation or a livelihood. It is the very basis of the village systems which, despite their serious drawbacks, provide the Indian society its resilience and tolerance. Hence, when they are pauperised, put in debt traps and forced to end their lives, legislators and economic planners should not be viewing them merely as an economic liability.

True to its characteristic reliance on propaganda, the regime made it appear that the farmers' agitation is fuelled by separatists and opposition parties. The genuine concerns of farmers were sidelined and ridiculed. Government spokespersons questioned the farmers' insistence on getting more than what they already get, in the form of cheap electricity and subsidised fertilisers. However, it is not the government that subsidises the farmers, it is the farmers who subsidise the nation by not demanding pension, old age allowance, annual increments and LTA. They are merely asking for guarantee that their produce gets a reasonable, minimum price.

Elaborate war-time debates are a distinct feature of epic poems. There are many debates within the Mahabharata— for instance, why could the war that destroyed a civilisation not be prevented in the first place? Many of those discussions point to the greed, contempt and anger of Duryodhana and to his father turning (literally) a blind eye to evil as possible explanations. The ancient Mahabharata provided space for a metaphysical text like Gita to exist. Anger towards all those who hold divergent views and contempt for constitutional norms are the unmistakable features of the present regime. The Constitution assures us that India is and will continue to be a democracy. The directive principles in it are clear about the direction in which state policies ought to move. Let us hope that the epic agitation by India's farmers instils in the regime a desire to stand by constitutional norms and not force a Mahabharata-like destruction.

Genes Inspected, Hate Word Resurrected

In September 2019, a research article with crucial relevance for South Asia was published in *Science* under the title 'The Formation of Human Populations in South and Central Asia' (*Science* Vol. 365, No. 6457). Dealing with the genetic study of several hundred 'ancient humans', the article was jointly authored by 108 collaborating scientists working in some of the best science institutions across more than twenty countries. It stated: 'The primary ancestral population of modern South Asians is a mixture of people related to early Holocene populations of Iran and South Asia that we detect in outlier individuals from two sites in cultural contact with the Indus Valley Civilization (IVC). After the IVC's decline, this population mixed with north-western groups with Steppe ancestry to form the "Ancestral North Indians" (ANI) and also mixed with south-eastern groups to form the "Ancestral South Indians".' The report led to further research by other scholars in archaeology and genetics over the last few years.

A report with such technical complexity and scientific depth normally tends to remain outside the horizon of interests of citizens. Yet, it acquires significance today, given that some deeply disturbing terms, discarded by the civilised world long ago, are being resurrected in India. The most crucial among these is the term 'pure'. On the face of it, it is not an offensive word. It can refer to any unadulterated variety of food or drink or jewellery metals. That indeed has been its meaning, in all domains of language except one. The exception is eugenics—a theory severely condemned as an 'immoral science'—where the term 'pure' and its antonym 'impure' are used as adjectives for 'blood', laying the foundation for racism.

In the German language of the 1930s, the term untermenschen—subhumans—was widely used for people other than those with 'pure-Aryan blood'. Nine decades later, the world is still not over the horror and tragedy wrought by the *untermenschen*-sociology. Its danger lay not just in being an unscientific idea or an immoral politics, but in becoming the theoretical handle that forced millions of innocent humans to concentration camps and mass graves. Johann Fitche's ideas of *Volkish nationalism*, eugenics applied to social restructuring, Hitler's storm troopers who made complete a mockery of any civilised law and the technological might of Germany were the four pillars that created Hitlerism.

The main justification provided by Hitler to justify his violence and cruelty was that the Serbs, Poles, Jews, Gypsies and Asians were not of 'pure Aryan blood', and therefore, did not deserve survival. Within two years of Hitler's coming to power, in May 1935, the Jews were banned entry into the armed forces and in September that year, the most shameful law for the 'Protection of German Blood and Honour' was passed. It criminalised intermarriages and sexual relations between the 'pure blood Germans' and the 'polluting' Jews. Shockingly though, the ugly term 'racial purity' found its resurrection in India in 2022. The Union Ministry of Culture put out—as the *New Indian Express* of 1 June reported—funds for DNA profiling kits and instruments for 'establishing the genetic history and trace the purity of races in India'. The scientist at the behest of whom the project was being launched stated: 'We want to see how mutation and mixing of genes in the Indian population has happened in the past 10,000 years.' He then went on to add, 'We will then have a clear cut idea of genetic history. You may even say that this will be an effort to trace the purity of races in India.' The Ministry of Culture quickly declared that the news was fake. The scientist in question distanced himself from the report by claiming that his words were wrongly reported. But, following the claim and the counter claim, a group of eminent scientists in India issued a statement warning that the notion of 'race' is dated and dangerous, and that genetics no longer looks at it as 'scientific'. The group that issued the statement included some of the most illustrious Indian scientists and historians. Chilling and completely out of sync with the Constitution of India as the idea is, what indeed can 'purity of races' mean in the Indian context? Would it be tied with the age-old caste system based on the fear of pollution, or is it trying to target the individuals who migrated to India during the medieval times? For it is no secret that the present regime does not need to depend on genetic tests to create second-class citizens; it has already invented its own ways to divide society.

One can get to the heart of the project by looking at the list of 'communities' that have been subjected to gene-testing. They are typically the 'language isolates'—as the

Nehalis in Buldhana district of Maharashtra, or the Adivasi such as the Jarwas and Nicobaris of Andaman Islands or the Malpahadis and Kondhs of Odisha. These precisely were the communities targeted two decades ago, when the multinational pharmaceutical companies were in search of 'un-adulterated cells'. That search proved a mere chimera. If genetics knows so, why go for the Adivasis again? The answer is, it is already well established that the different populations in India have claim to a shared mitochondrial DNA, the one inherited from the mother's side. Using this already known scientific fact, the Ministry of Culture's project can easily result in ruling out the Adivasis as the sole first inhabitants of the subcontinent. That will clear the path for propagating the unscientific claim that the imagined pre-Harappan Sanskrit speaking people migrated from India westward to the rest of Asia and towards the north into the steppes. The RSS view of history is obsessively interested in proving that Sanskrit was in use since the Indus Valley civilisation. This view, entirely unsupported by scientific evidence, claims Sanskrit initially emerged in India and then spread out in the rest of the world, and that many languages outside India have Sanskrit as their ancestor.

For half a century before Hitler came to power, similar arguments were put forward regarding the imagined prehistoric home of the Aryans. The game this time is the same, even as a group of more than hundred accomplished scientists have already exposed the absurdity of the claim. The regime has built for its cultural narrative a castle of sand. Is the Ministry of Culture building a pseudo-scientific showcase for it? Apart from denying Adivasis their cultural space and science its legitimacy, this move will also legitimise social disharmony between the so-called pure and the so-called impure citizens.

As genes get inspected and words get resurrected, the guarantee of equal citizenship given by the Constitution may get mired in hatred and stark injustice. 'Pure' is not an innocent adjective. It can turn vicious when applied to race.

Let us hope the Ministry of Culture publicly assures Indians that it will not be party to an idea which deserves no place in civilised society.

Pegasus, Equus and Horse Trading

The Economist Intelligence Unit (EIU) brings out an Annual Democracy Index. The report for 2020 puts India two places down, from the 51st to the 53rd. It takes no more than one's horse sense to realise that the idea of democracy in India is under siege. To citizens struggling to survive in their daily grind, this is no news; and we hardly need an EIU Index to tell us how bad things have been, for that is no Greek and Latin. Yet, a new Greek and Latin connection on the horizon has turned a quotidian reality into intriguing news. The news is not about horse play in the Parliament, nor about horse trading in state assemblies, but just about horses—mythical and historical.

Gods are a product of the human imagination, though in ancient civilisations, gods were believed to have preceded humans and to possess supernatural forms and qualities. They could undertake cosmic adventures, and could also commit terrible blunders. The ancient Greeks had imagined their gods to be quite like themselves, most of them prone to foibles and frailties. Poseidon, from the Greek pantheon, lived on the Mount Olympus and was regarded as the lord of seas. Myth depicts him in an overwhelmingly white colour, with a strikingly well-kempt white beard. Myths about him tell us that he fathered two horses. Areion—a ferociously fast horse—was born out of his pursuit of Demeter. The other he sired with the Gorgon Medusa. Medusa was a winged female who held poisonous, living snakes in her hair. Their offspring had a white mane like his father's beard, and wings like his mother. Its name was Pegasus. Having been in oblivion for three thousand years, Pegasus is back in news, thousands of miles away from Greece, in Bharat.

The Latin term for horse was 'equus'. It was used for all kinds of horse-like species including donkeys and zebras. In sharp contrast with the deadly horses of the Greek mythology, the Latin 'equus' was just an herbivore, a pure vegetarian type, all its females ready to accept the mastery of a single stallion lording over mares in a defined territory. At least some of the equus varieties were domesticated by humans. Domestication of horses began in Ukraine and Kazakhstan around 4000 BC. Over the next two thousand years, horse domestication was a part of human life. Archaeological finds in Sintashta and Petrovka show horses buried in graves around 2000 BC. Genetic research points to the possibility of the entire 'horse population' having sprung up from a single sub-group—haplotype—of the genus Equus. All of this information could not be more irrelevant for a society battling COVID, unemployment, astronomical prices, lack of personal safety, collapse of democratic institutions and intimidation from all directions. Yet it is the malware sold 'only to governments' by a company named NSO-Group, registered in Israel by Omri Lavie, Shalev Hulio and Niv Carmi, that has brought back Pegasus into TV news rooms, print media and, by extension, the drawing rooms of Indians. And, it is the unusually virulent attack by the RSS historians on the 'Western', 'Marxist' and 'anti-national' historians that has brought back 'Equus' into webinars and torrents of misinformation on WhatsApp.

Reports say that when a sustained campaign of horse trading was unleashed under the title 'Operation Lotus' in order to topple a democratically formed government in Karnataka, phone numbers of G. Parameshwar (ex-Deputy CM), personal secretaries of Siddaramaiah (ex-CM) and H.D. Kumaraswamy (ex-CM), were sent to Pegasus for targeting the political stables and their stability. The modern avatar of the winged sea-horse was let loose on not just many 'namdharis' but a few 'kamdharis' as well. And since the Constitution of India has provided us with the three wings of authorities, the two-winged horse was asked to snoop on mighty persons in the executive, the legislative and the judiciary, so true to the word of the Constitution!

Moving from the Greek to the Latin horse, one must say that never before in the entire Indian history has the question acquired so much significance as to whether horses slipped into India from outside, bringing a new language, a different oral poetry and culture to the north-west India, or if they galloped out from India and established their mastery over the entire 'old world', spreading the language of their indigenous Aryan masters. All of the research on evolution of the equus species flies in the face of the 'indigenous Aryans' hypothesis. But a chance horse tooth found in the late Harappan cultural period has rekindled the hopes of those who believe that emergence of Sanskrit pre-dates the historical slot provided for it by the international community of researchers, linguists, archaeologists and historians. This right-wing historiography is keen on establishing that the Saraswati-Sindhu river culture is the cradle in which Vedic wisdom started sprouting. If this can be established to be 'logical', the question of the outsider/insider in the Hindu Rashtra can be settled with an ease that a sharp knife has in slicing fresh butter. Horse, equus, chariot, weapons, wars, language are all materials of the narrative that can sanitise Indian pre-history and ensconce it cosily on the throne of Hinduism. The simple difficulty is that in doing so, the number of non-scientific assumptions, evidence and conclusions that will crowd the conception of the Indian past will be similar to the Aegean Stables that Hercules had to clean.

The twentieth-century world has already been witness to the lengths nationalism seen in terms of genetic purity can go and the ignominy that the 'others' have to endure. The compact of Hindutva with an engineered view of history implies the blending of a theocratic state and a racist politics. It would serve us well if we recall that the sacrifice of the martyrs of the freedom struggle was aimed at leading India into a democratic universe of freedom, social harmony and equality of citizenship rights. Not, on the other hand, to bring about an ashwa-yuga—an era of snooping horses, fabulated horse-histories and horse-trading—no matter what the neighing in manufactured consent-factories on WhatsApp want us to believe.

Between *Nakba* and *Nauba*

The attack by Israel on 15 May 2021 on the Al Jala building in which, among other residents and offices, the Al Jazeera's offices too were situated, was widely denounced by citizens, the press, international agencies and media organisations all over the world. The entire multi-storied building came tumbling down, leaving many dead and wounded. The media house, Al Jazeera, was given barely an hour's notice to vacate it before the attack was made. The heinous act has its roots in a seventy-three-year-old decision to create Israel as a country for Jews who had been without a homeland for centuries. The idea of a Jew-homeland, Zion, was articulated by Theodor Herzl in his book *Der Judenstaat* (1896), which soon became the early twentieth century credo for Zionism. It was in May 1948 that Israel was carved out as a country for Jews from all over the world, leading to the forced displacement of nearly seven lakh Arabs.

This phenomenon, of forcing countless people out of their homes to create a home for a group who had been historically homeless and scattered, was captured in the popular imagination by the Arabic term 'nakba'. It means a great catastrophe or a phenomenal disaster. Initially, the term was used from the perspective of the Palestinian Arabs. Subsequently, as conflict between the Palestinian Arabs and the Israeli Jews acquired other local tones and a different texture in international diplomacy, the term was pressed into service to depict, quite ironically, the plight of Israeli victimhood. Today *nakba* or *naxba*, spelt both ways, is not understood exclusively as either Arab victimhood or Israeli victimhood.

15 May, which marks the anniversary of the Nakba, was chosen for the attack so that it sent out a clear message to the world. The symbolism was not about the selfhood of a Jew homeland. It was, unfortunately, more about the ascendency of right-wing politics. It was about the normalisation of violence and genocide; and it was also about twisting history in which dominance by force itself is moral validation for action. It is sad, though not surprising, that Zionism has been held by the RSS as worthy of emulation in India in its desire to convert it into a Hindu Rashtra. The Arabic word *Naxba* brings to one's mind another Arabic term *Nauba*. That too means a catastrophe, a disaster, or a situation or condition inviting catastrophe. The Arabic *Nauba* in time became *naubat* in Persian and is in use in Hindi, Marathi and Gujarati with similar meanings. However, while *nakba* refers to the silent pain and suffering caused by a numbing catastrophe, *nauba* brings home woe and wailing in anticipation of an impending catastrophe.

The entire months of April and May 2021 were characteristic of an unparalleled *naubat* in India. Switch on a TV channel, open a newspaper or magazine, or pick up the phone and call a friend, you noticed this shroud of *naubat* enveloping the words that come to you. Quite clearly, we were in the middle of a calamity, the scale of which had no precedence in known history. The pandemic had so far affected nearly three crore persons. Nearly four lakh new cases were being reported daily. One was hoping that this number did not rise to seven or eight lakh by mid-June as was being predicted by experts. We were not thinking of the third phase of the pandemic as yet, though there was a clear indication that another deadly phase may affect India.

Some recent media investigations indicate that the actual number of causalities in the second phase of the pandemic is many times more than the official numbers being put out; but even the compacted official statistics are frightening. The figures are larger or at par with the figures of victims in the disastrous natural or man-made calamities in the past. The Spanish Flu in 1918-19 affected seventeen million persons. The Partition of India and Pakistan resulted in the death of one to two million persons. The Bangladesh war saw 2,69,000 persons killed in the subcontinent, including Pakistanis, Indians and Bangladeshis. The Killari earthquake killed over thirty thousand and the Kutch earthquake took 18,600 lives. The official death toll of the pandemic has crossed the three lakh mark, with the number of affected persons being over 3 crore. This, without taking into account records of crematoria or the corpses fished out of rivers.

The corona spate was to intensify as weeks passed. One simply did not know then how disastrous it would be if the dreaded third phase hit us. The tribal and rural districts, which had so far remained relatively unaffected by the pandemic, had started showing a high incidence of COVID. Millions of families had lost their dear ones, jobs and hope. And the biological corona epidemic was, sadly, coupled with an ideological corona. What we were facing was not just an individual's tragedy. It is a large, unprecedented and universal catastrophe, a *nakba* or a *nauba*.

What is shocking is that the central government had not just been ineffective in coping with the catastrophe, but even cynical in its approach. No prime minister of a country with a population of 135 crore people living in extremely crowded cities and towns would have kept the pandemic management deliberately on hold in view of a foreign dignitary visit in March 2020. No PM would have allowed, encouraged and actively sponsored huge election rallies and religious *mela*s knowing that the second wave had already set in. No one, except the most callous, would have allowed the vaccine producing companies to export vaccines when the requirement at home was so overwhelming; and no regime would have put out fake narratives accusing the Tablighi gathering to be the source of all trouble.

While scientists all over the world were working round the clock to find a fool-proof response to the threat of corona, the regime had been busy undermining scientific thought. I wrote these words in pain, not in anger. Every home in the nation was dealing with the death of a loved one. Death surrounded us. One felt sad at the thought that when the new grand parliament building came into being, the first meeting held there may turn out to be one for national mourning. When the Ayodhya temple came into existence and was opened for worship, the first expression may—I hoped not—be 'Hey Ram'. What an unprecedented *nauba*, biological and ideological!

A Father and Three Daughters

THE WORLD IS INDEED A SMALL PLACE. IF NOT, WHY WOULD the recently devastated Ukrainian Poltava create a familiar echo in Karnataka's Shivamoga? There is apparently no connection between the Poltava city along the Vorskla river and Shivamoga along the Tunga and the Bhadra. Then, why would a twelfth-century story of insanity and love from a distant island come to visit Karnataka in the twenty-first century, transcending a span of a millennium and a distance of several continents?

The story involves three daughters and their doting, old father. It was reported first by the twelfth-century historian Geoffrey of Monmouth. The story was then reproduced by Raphael Holinshed during the sixteenth century. A century later, William Shakespeare employed it as the plot for his tragedy *King Lear*. Since then, Shakespeare's tragedy has not ceased to inspire writers all over the world. One of them was a nineteenth-century genius from Poltava in central Ukraine. Born in 1859, Solomon Naumovich belonged to the minority within the Ashkenazi Jewish community. When he started writing during his teens, he took the pen-name Sholem Aleichem. Shakespeare's story of Lear and his three daughters appealed to him as it was similar to his engagement with three languages—Russian, Hebrew and Yiddish. Of these three, he gave up on the first two and passionately kept up with Yiddish. Though deeply influenced by Germanic languages, Yiddish had kept alive its links with Hebrew and Arabic.

Solomon's pen-name, Sholam Aleichem, reminiscent of the Arabic 'Salaam Alequm', takes one back to the ancient Hebrew 'Sholem', closely linked in its linguistic genesis with what Sanskrit inherited as 'Shanti', both having roots in ancient Indo-Iranian. Sholem Aleichem's rendering of the story had the king turned into an amusing milkman called Tevey. Given that he was witnessing the rise of a bitter anti-Semitic social ethos in Eastern Europe, his fiction got suffused with the pain and anxiety predicting the impending holocaust. Like many other Jews of his day, he chose to migrate to the US when the First World War began. It was his fiction that inspired Joseph Stein to produce his musical *Fiddler on the Roof*, later made into a film by the same title.

The songs of Stein's superlative musical thrilled the world and the depiction of religious discrimination made him a hero in the fight against anti-Semitism. It would have been a surprise had Stein's movie not attracted Jayant Kaikini, one of the finest lyricists of India in our time. Kaikini, son of a major Kannada fiction writer Gourish Kaikini, grew up in a progressive atmosphere and after a spell in Bombay's industrial ethos, took to writing himself. He has produced an outstanding collection of fiction, poetry and plays, has won many literary awards and is held today as a leading Indian writer and lyricist writing in Kannada.

Jayant Kaikini's *Jathegiruvanu Chandira* (*The Moon Will be with Us*) was published as part of a collection of his plays a decade and half ago. It has been performed in Bangalore and elsewhere and has received laurels for its control of language and dramatic intensity. It was performed in Shivamoga by the theatre group Rangabelaku led by Kotrappa S. Hiremagadi. When a performance was staged, it was disrupted by Bajarang Dal members. Their argument was that the place where it was being performed was a Veershaiva hall, and to perform a play with a Muslim character in it would be sacrilege. Little do the Bajrang Dal members know that the Ukrainian author who created the modern story of the kind milkman and his three daughters had a name which literally means 'Peace be on you', which in its Sanskrit form is 'Shanti, Shanti, Shanti', the ultimate benediction for every Upanishad.

One wonders whether the disruptors know at all that the founding text of the Veershaiva sect, the *Shri Sidhanta Shikhamani*, states, '*Bhaavo Yasy sthiro nityam manovaakkyaayakarmabhi … shaanto daantstapashishilah satyavaak samadarshan*' meaning, 'Do hold the 'Shiv—bhava'—the mentality inspired by the divine—as the primary duty; do learn the 'shant' (peace), generosity, study, truthful speech, for they are manifestation of the divine'. The truth is the vandals who disrupted the performance hardly care for the teachings of the Veershaiva path of life, nor do they know the long trajectory of the story that Kaikini's play brought to the Shivamoga performance. Vandalism and cultural suppression are tragically short of memory. They may act in the name of tradition, but they barely have any knowledge of what they are defending. The finest theatre academy in the country created by Subanna is located at Heggodu in Shimoga district. Prasanna, another accomplished playwright and director, is resident in the same district. The people in the district have seen some of the greatest theatre productions over the last fifty years. It is difficult to imagine that theatre would be brought under attack there. Sadly, Shimoga has not been spared from the cultural vandalism let loose on India as a whole.

In today's India, Hindutva forces have little time to understand what Hindu philosophies and metaphysics actually propagate. Sholem, being an Ashkenazim, understood how the hatred for Jews in Europe during the late nineteenth century was affecting the creative sources of Russia, Germany and France. The case of Dreyfus imprisonment and trial is still not forgotten. Defenders of human dignity such as Sarah Bernhardt, Anatole France, Georges Clemenceau and Emile Zola have not been pushed into oblivion. The hatred for Jews in Russia, France and in Hitler's Germany is remembered till date as shameful episodes in history.

In recent years, several important writers in Karnataka such as U.R. Ananthamurthy, Girish Karnad, Devanoor Mahadeva and Rahmat Tarikere have spoken against the rising atmosphere of hatred. Some, like M.M. Kalburgi and Gauri Lankesh had to face bullets. Initially, it was an apprehension, a view of a horizon turning dark with clouds. Then followed physical assaults. The state actively ignited and encouraged an anti-minority sentiment. Now, the hatred project is on auto-pilot. It no longer requires state patronage or concealment of its intentions through subterfuge. The drama unfolding before the people of India is supported by an indulgent state, with the RSS, Vishva Hindu Parishad (VHP) and Bajrang Dal as its eager actors. The theatre of hatred has made spectacular progress. It has declared that even an imaginary character in a play can pollute the purity of a religious place. It will not be surprising that all of this is in preparation for a project that aims to assess the racial purity of citizens. The world has always been a small place; India, however, is becoming far smaller than what our rapidly disappearing Constitution had imagined it to be.

What Is Staring India in the Face

In several Indian languages, the term for a deeply enigmatic question is 'yaksh-prashn'. The term draws upon the Mahabharata where Dharma, also known as Yudhishtir, had to answer a series of difficult moral and metaphysical questions posed by his father Yama. Dharma managed to satisfy Yama through his thoughtful answers, and eventually the Pandavas emerged triumphant during the Kurukshetra war. In our time, several yaksha questions staring India in the face call for answers. Here is a random list of some urgent and intriguing questions.

1. Who does not know that the rich have become super-rich and the poor have been pauperised? The working classes work more and yet continue to receive less in return. Inflation is increasing by the day and employment opportunities have gone down. All material conditions clearly indicate a social explosion. Yet, is it that people who are crushed by material deprivation have chosen to suffer deprivation, rather than challenge the vast disparity?

2. While governments are busy clamping down on the rights of individuals, why is it that the citizens continue to return the same political party to power which would serve to further reduce the citizens' right of choice? Anti-people policies are being actively imposed on the nation, why do people not express their dissatisfaction with their representatives who have failed to represent people's aspirations?
3. If media was seen in the past as one of the pillars of democracy, and if democracy is indeed the system that we believe operates in our country, why is the media caving in? If speaking truth to power spells out the very reason for the media's existence, why is it that it is seen doing everything else but speaking truth? When mediapersons try to do so, and if as a result they are assassinated or imprisoned, why do their colleagues prefer to remain silent?
4. India became a nation after a long struggle for freedom which required great sacrifice and hard work to transform our society from its medieval biases to a modern and egalitarian outlook. Why it is that people are ready to give up the hard-won freedom and modernity and choose to slide back to superstition, fantasy and bravado characteristic of the medieval ages? Why do people respond to calls for banging *thali*s and clapping during a pandemic that has to be countered through scientific temper? Why is it that in less than three quarters of a century, the citizens have turned away from the memories of the freedom struggle? Why are they lavishing praises on those who helped the colonial masters while lampooning those who faced gallows, bullets and prisons? Why do we treat violation of privacy of individuals and pervasive state surveillance as matters not worthy of concern?

5. How and why have we got intoxicated in the name of religion? Why have we turned to avenging blunders of rulers long gone? Why do we so easily get angry with our fellow citizens? Why do we take the accident of someone's birth in a given religion as a mark of her or his criminality and join mobs in acts of lynching? Heterodoxy marked India's history for several millennia. In the past, we accepted worshipping many gods. Why are we projecting theological and sectarian identity as the primary identity of people? Why has the worst orthodoxy so suddenly replaced the ideas propagated by a long line of saints and Sufis? Why are we so keen on negating spirituality and projecting the mere outer forms of religion? Why have we forgotten the essence of scriptures while claiming to fight in the name of god?
6. Our nation took birth as a republic, as a union of states, with a well laid out division of authority in various matters. Then, how have we allowed ourselves to become an increasingly unitary nation and the Centre to become increasingly indifferent to the space of the states? When earlier diversity was accepted as the foundation of India, how is it that we have developed such contempt for cultural, linguistic and religious difference? Why are we so intolerant of diverse dress codes, food habits, diverse views and cultural backgrounds of the people of India?
7. Though the segregation of the legislative, judiciary and executive has been unambiguously worked out in the constitution, why has the bureaucracy caved in and why is the judiciary not maintaining its independence? When defence forces are devised to keep themselves completely above sectarian politics, how is that they too appear to have imbibed elements of communalism? Why it is that

institutions that should work as watchdogs for keeping governments within constitutional boundaries have developed a competitive affinity to the ruling regime? Why do we not have enough officers and high functionaries who can reverse the partisan use of agencies?

8. While India has several hundred universities, higher education institutions and scientific bodies, why have they not succeeded in developing a critique of the system? Why do they not raise questions that will serve our democracy and work in the interest of the life and rights of our people? Why are they found almost absent on the national scene when required to defend reason, sanity, compassion and empathy?

One can go on adding to these questions. We may brush aside a majority of them by pointing out that they are not peculiar to India, for the situation is no different in many other countries. One may also point to similar instances from earlier decades, by taking recourse to 'what about then?' Yet, none of these TV-studio tactics can help wish them away. The mythical Dharma had a series of snap replies ready in his moral and metaphysical armour. For us, if we do offer answers, those answers in turn may beg a series of counter questions. Yet, these questions must be tackled if India has to survive as a modern democracy and republic.

People in general tend to believe that the Constitution of India which we accepted as India's 'dharma' is still in force, even if the letters in it have acquired greater value than the spirit behind them. Alas, the irony is that the Constitution, which should have weaned people away from their fatalism and brought them closer to a vibrant understanding of their rights and responsibilities, seems itself to suffer at the hands of fatalistic indifference. People appear to have adopted a resigned attitude, a fatalistic stamina to wait for a change to fall from the skies.

The time has come for each one of us to remind ourselves that since Independence, the Constitution is our primary dharma. India cannot allow it to be replaced with any text like *Manusmriti*, which seeks to justify caste differences as divine retribution. The Constitution is at present under siege by a non-state-actor organisation on the one hand and a greed-driven corporates on the other. Therefore, a free and fearless expression becomes our only instrument of change, and the polar star for India's future. To believe in the inviolable supremacy of the Constitution is for us the only way to recover the idea of India.

The Mother of Democracy

THE TWENTY-FIRST CENTURY WORLD IS EXTREMELY different from the twentieth century world. The nature of individualism has changed over the last hundred years. The characteristics of 'capital' have changed. The complexities of urban settlements have changed too. Yet, any attempt at understanding the unrestrained state and the global menace of totalitarianism in the present time can happen only by taking into consideration their twentieth century manifestations. Several important thinkers since the times of Adolf Hitler and Joseph Stalin have thought about the genesis of totalitarianism and the acceptance of dictatorial leaders by the people they govern. Among those thinkers, Hannah Arendt (1906–1975) is perhaps the most important. Having seen the mindless violence of the Second World War and the inhuman treatment of Jews, Poles, Gypsies and the coloured population in the Third Reich, as well as having thought deeply about the Stalinist liquidations of large numbers in the USSR and destruction of millions of peasants, Arendt developed a matchless inwardness to the psychology and politics of totalitarian regimes. In her landmark books *The Origins of Totalitarianism* (1951) and *The Human Condition* (1958), she presented an acute analysis of twentieth-century totalitarianism, which she clearly distinguished from the feudal violence and wars of the past era. She showed how the twentieth-century totalitarianism was founded on terror and, more importantly, on ideological fiction. The new totalitarian state was, in her opinion, brought to life through manufacturing a sense of great historical injustice and insult and promising retribution and revenge through semi-formal mobs acting in the name of the state. It lured masses—for whom the Supreme Leader had nothing but disdain—by promising to change the status of the majority community from that of 'historically offended' to that of 'being capable of offending'. The majority community, lured by these promises, were ready to offend the imagined past offenders even without any explicit command from the Leader. Providing 'the key to unlock history' to the nation, because the nation was 'the chosen one', was the stated life-mission of the Leader. His terror-generating authority extended to claiming that he was specially born to achieve the majority community's vengeful goal. They applauded him, knowing well that his actions hurt them, destroyed their families and engulfed the society in an atmosphere of ever-growing hatred.

The world knows how the Supreme Leaders of the hatred-driven totalitarian states of the twentieth century were ultimately brought down, and the shame that is still attached to their memory. Yet, in less than a century, the totalitarian state has made its reappearance all over the world. The phenomenon cannot be understood merely by placing them in the 'right' or the 'left' political categories, nor can their essential nature be fully grasped by looking at them merely as an extension of the gluttonous corporate capitalism. It is necessary to add that the twenty-first century brand of totalitarianism is aided by the new challenge arising from artificial intelligence; but that is only a part of the problem.

Mattias Desmet, from Belgium's Ghent University, has now come up with an explanation of the widespread totalitarianism in the twenty-first century. In his recently published work, *The Psychology of Totalitarianism* (published by Chelsea Green in 2022), which is available in English translation now, Desmet proposes that people all over the world are gripped by irreversible loneliness (a point drawn upon Arendt), and have rendered themselves incapable of facing risks. The craving for risk-prevention and risk-mitigation has become, in his view, a pervasive tendency. He calls it the 'insurance syndrome', with normalisation of not just the insurance of life and assets, but also an 'insurance of insurance'. Desmet argues that citizens now look up to the state for imposing regulations on them in the hope of making life risk-free. In such a situation, a clever politician can rise to the top by creating a fear of attacks by unnamed 'enemies' (terrorists, aliens or even viruses) and then by promising protection to citizens by imposing stringent regulations. In the process, the privacy, autonomy and sanctity of individuals get sacrificed. The state comes to be seen as far more important than the traditional rights of individuals. The twenty-first century brand of totalitarianism too grabs control over populations in the name of protecting the majority; and it too demonises minorities. Through a discussion of the coronavirus epidemic and the related regulations in various countries, Desmet demonstrates that the social and political cost of remedy for prevention and mitigation of risks can often be much higher than the costs people would have paid had they faced the risks by themselves. In short, while the twentieth-century totalitarianism emerged from the perceived sense of historical injustice, its twenty-first century counterpart is born out of people's perceived sense of isolation and fear and their utter unwillingness to face risks. The violence unleashed by dictators in the previous century was more tangible and more scarlet in colour. However, the violence perpetrated by today's Supreme Leaders is not just blood-soaked. It is generated in cold regulations imposed by the technocratic state, justified by the large-scale manufacture of entirely fictitious data.

We are coming to the end of the first quarter of the twenty-first century. We know that like all regimes in the past, the current regime in India too will be a story of the past—although we don't know when or how soon. But, after it is over, scholars of political history will definitely think about the genesis and the exact nature of totalitarianism that India has faced since 2014. Quite likely, they will notice that the Indian variety had a strange mixture of the peculiarities of the twentieth-century totalitarianism as well as the twenty-first-century totalitarianism. In India, many centuries live together in every form of our life—in our expression of freedom as well as in the way we face domination, patriarchy, discrimination and dictatorships. The works of Arendt and Desmet can help us understand how and where those who claim India to be the mother of democracy have brought the mother and the daughter, leaving them standing today in fear and agony.

What the Thunder Said

IN 1922, A THIRTY-YEAR-OLD ENGLISH POET, WHO WAS LATER awarded the Nobel Prize for literature, wrote a long poem, a modern-day epic by common consent. More than a century later, Eliot's *The Waste Land* resonates for us in India, not because of its prophecy or irony, its allusions to Dante, Shakespeare and Buddha, or its use of Greek, Latin and Sanskrit terms, but because of a curious tale it picked up from the *Brihad Aranyaka*. The *Arnyaka*, the earliest among the Upanishads, is a treasure trove of mythical stories. One of these appears in the fifth section of *The Waste Land*, titled 'What the Thunder Said'.

This is how it goes: After Prajapati, the maker of the world, had created beings and things, he danced in frenzy and kept shouting '*da, da da …*' Ecstasy over, he assembled his progeny—the devas, the danavas and the manavas—and asked if they had understood what he had said. The *deva*s, replied, '*da* is *damyata*': 'learn self-control'; the *manava*s thought he had said, '*datta*': 'learn to overcome greed'; the *danava*s said, '*dayadhvam*', 'learn to forgive'. Prajapati laughed enigmatically and said, 'Well, you seem to have understood perhaps.'

Without forgetting that this is but an old myth and not to be mistaken for history, I have often wondered, if there is a single moment in the known history of India when the *praja* has danced in ecstasy, as did Prajapati in mythical times, to celebrate an essential creation. I like to believe that the 26 November 1949 was that moment—when we, the people, adopted, enacted and gave unto ourselves the Constitution. It ignited a hope in the mind of every Indian, which no moment in the past had achieved. More than seventy years later, what diverse responses does it evoke now?

Remembering the day, the constitutional head of India's judiciary said that the 'citizenry of independent India' has breathed life into 'what might otherwise have been just another bare document'. Many of our freedom fighters, as he reminded the nation, were lawyers—including Gandhi, Ambedkar, Nehru, Lajpat Rai, Patel and Alladi Krishnaswamy Iyer. His appreciation of litigants, judges, law-makers and lawyers reminded the country that it is the people who matter above all. The response to the *Samvidhan Divas* by the principal opposition party was to remind the Prime Minister that the institutions envisioned by the Constitution have been rendered dysfunctional during his regime and 'the constitution was being undermined every day'. The thoughts of the Prime Minister on the day revolved round his pet theme of dynastic politics as a threat to democracy, colonial mindset and 'misuse' of the freedom enshrined in the Constitution as hindrance to the country's development. His irritation towards those he thinks hinder development was clear in word and tone.

All three paid their homage to the martyrs who sacrificed lives in order to win India freedom. Influenced by visuals in films, emotive theatre, stories heard from elders and distorted snippets coming through social media, the nation's memory of the freedom struggle is quite truncated. Who remembers today, for instance, the names of the thousands of young people of the 1940s, who plunged into the Quit India and Civil Disobedience Movement, faced the gallows, were shot by the colonial police or rotted in jail? Who remembers the tribes and castes that fought British rule in villages and cities right from the Santal rising in the 1850s to the year of independence in 1947?

Let me mention in brief just one of those many struggles towards India's freedom struggle. It is the 'Battle of Aberdeen', a violent clash between the 'convicts' deported by the British to the Penal Colony in Andaman after 1857 and the native Adivasi population of the islands. Anthropologist Vishwajit Pandya tells us that in April 1859, a batch of Indian prisoners had escaped the Penal Settlement and wanted to hide in the habitat of the Adivasis. They killed all but one, realising that the convicts had been clearing the forest to create British settlements. A month later, in May 1859, the Adivasis decided to attack the British establishment; but one of the 'convicts'— Dudhnath Tiwari, convict no. 276—whom they had not killed, betrayed them and reported the plot to British officers. As a result, the group of fifteen hundred tribal men had to face bullets fired from the navy schooner Charlotte. Why had the convicts attempted an escape? Just a year ago, on 18 May 1858, on a single day, scores of prisoners had been hanged— twenty-six of them deported from the Bombay Presidency alone and most in their early twenties. One finds in the record of martyrs documented by the Indian Council for Historical Research that among those who were deported to Andaman from the erstwhile Bombay Presidency, a total of thirty-seven were hanged. They belonged to all castes and religions. Of the thirty-seven, fourteen were Muslims. This does not apply only to the 1857 resistance to the British rule—throughout the long history of the Indian freedom struggle, women and men from all castes, communities, religions and regions risked their lives to build a free and forward-looking India. Historical records show that some esoteric groups did not participate in the freedom struggle, some individuals accepted to submit mercy petitions and yet others became informants to the British rulers. However, the tribal communities, workers, peasants, students and common people braved imprisonment or bullets and fought to build a free nation that will ensure justice, freedom and equality. The Constitution was and remains the culmination of the struggle.

Returning to the *Aranyaka* myth, one tends to agree with the Chief Justice of India that the people have kept the Constitution alive, despite 'clean chits' to architects of riots and FIRs against victims of atrocities. One agrees with opposition parties that democratic institutions have crumbled—outside as well inside the political parties. Yes, the Prime Minister was right in pointing to 'family-centric' action as a hindrance to development. Indeed, catering to only a few corporate families has caused a grave economic crisis for the rest of India.

One wonders if, like the mythical Prajapati, the *praja* could laugh, for it knows that the creation of the Constitution does not guarantee its sustenance. Surely, it is bearing witness, through the millions of eyes that made it.

Must Every Elephant Cease to Be?

The Bengali writer Mahasweta Devi has a story titled 'Death of Jagmohan, the Elephant'. The death of an elephant strikes us as a rather 'big death'. She wanted to say that there are many invisible deaths. They include deaths of dalits and tribals trapped in hunger and humiliation. Anonymity surrounds them, and our lack of compassion gives their silent burial a finality. The death of a tree or a forest sacrificed on the altar of development is mourned, but not spoken about. The death of a language is surrounded in silence. By its very nature, it cannot be visible, and so it fails to move anyone, except the very last speaker of the language, who nurtures an unrequited hope of response. When a language dies, it leaves forever, taking with it the knowledge gathered over centuries. With it sinks a unique world view. We fail to realise that this too is violence. Violence does not necessarily need physical action to manifest itself. Just as silence is an eloquent expression of love, an unstated thought can be a terrifying method for violence. More of culture and life get exterminated through slight shifts in policy instruments than through armed conflicts. It does not always take an all sweeping tsunami to annihilate a natural creation. A bureaucrat's benign decision can as well cause it. Even a well-intentioned language census can do it.

Over the last eighty plus years, successive governments have carried out a decadal census. The 1931 Census was quite a landmark as it held a clear mirror before the country about its caste and community composition. The year 1941 was an exception as war disrupted the exercise, and 1951 was a rather busy year for the new Indian republic. It was during the 1961 Census that languages in the country were enumerated fully. India learnt through it that a total of 1,652 mother tongues were being spoken in the country. Through a rather ill-founded logic, this figure was pegged in the 1971 Census at only 109—a reduction of 1,543. The logic was that a language deserved respectability only if it had more than ten thousand speakers. On no scientific grounds is it a fair decision; but it has stuck and the practice continues to be followed.

Language enumeration takes place in the first year of every decade. The data collected is disclosed to the public some six or seven years later. This is because the processing of language data is far more time-consuming than processing economic or other scientific data. In 2018, the Census of India declared the language data of the 2011 Census. The scale of the entire exercise is simply unprecedented, taking into account 120 crore speakers covering a very large number of languages. The language division of the Census office therefore deserves applause. Yet, the data presented leaves one with more questions than before.

During the census, the citizens of India responded with 19,569 distinct mother tongues. In technical terms, these are called 'raw returns'. Based on previously available linguistic and sociological information, the authorities decided that out of these, 18,200 did not 'logically' match with known information. A total of 1,369 names ('labels' as they are technically called) were identified as 'being names of languages'. The 'raw returns' left out represent nearly 60 lakh citizens. Thanks to the classification protocol, their linguistic citizenship got axed.

Then, in addition to the 1,369 'mother tongue' names shortlisted after scrutiny, there were 1,474 other mother tongue names which were placed under the generic label 'Others'. The census does not consider these linguistic 'others' to be their concern. They have languages of their own. They speak; but the classification system could not identify their languages. They are simply silenced by slapping an apparently innocuous label on them—Others!

The fortunate 1,369 were further grouped together under a total of 121 'group labels'. These are presented to the country as 'Languages'. Of these, twenty-two are languages included in the eighth schedule of the Constitution and referred to as the 'scheduled languages'. The remaining ninety-nine are described as the 'non-scheduled' languages. A closer look will make one realise that most of the groupings are forced. For instance, under the heading 'Hindi', there are nearly fifty other languages. Bhojpuri—spoken by more than 5 crore people, with its own cinema, theatre, literature, vocabulary and style—is grouped under 'Hindi'. Nearly 3 crore people from Rajasthan, with their own independent languages too, are shown as speaking Hindi as their mother tongue. The Powari/Pawri of the tribals in Maharashtra and Madhya Pradesh has been hitched to Hindi. So is the Kumauni of Uttarakhand. The report states that 52,83,47,193 speak Hindi as their mother tongue. And this simply is not so. A similarly inflated figure is given for Sanskrit by counting the returns given against the question about 'second language'. English is not considered for data relating to second language. Counting for it is restricted to the 'mother tongue' category, bringing down its numbers substantially. Considering the widespread use of English in education, law, administration, media and healthcare, a very significant number of Indians use English as a utility language. To some extent, it has also been the language of integration for our multilingual country. Is not the census required to capture that reality? It can, given the data on the language of second preference that it has; but it does not, for reasons that need no spelling out. And so, the census tells us that a total of 2,59,678 Indians speak English as their 'mother tongue'. Numerically accurate, semantically disastrous!

The language census may not attract as much attention as the rise and fall of diesel prices. But in the community of nations, the Census of India is bound to be discussed. A body like the UNESCO will look at it with interest. From its General Council's decision in 1946 to establish a Translation Bureau to the Executive Board's debate on 'Multilingualism in the Context of Education for All' held in October 2008, UNESCO has progressively developed its vision and deepened its understanding of global linguistic diversity. From time to time, it tries to highlight the key role that language plays in widening access to education, protecting livelihoods and in preserving culture and knowledge traditions. In 2000, UNESCO declared 21 February as International Mother Language Day, and in 2001 the 'Universal Declaration on Cultural Diversity' accepted the principle of 'Safeguarding the linguistic heritage of humanity and giving support to expression, creation and dissemination in the greatest possible number of languages'. Towards this end, UNESCO has launched the linguistic diversity network, supported research and brought out the *Atlas of World's Endangered Languages*, conceptualised a normative framework for measuring endangerment, and highlighted the central place of language in the world's intangible heritage. Is our language census consistent with these ideas and principles?

One expects that the census should, in the least, adequately reflect the linguistic composition of the country. Giving cold figures that help no one—educators, policymakers or the speakers of languages themselves—is a practice that deserves to be dated. The massive exercise, consuming immense time and energy, needs to update itself to enable greater inclusion of the marginal communities so that our intangible heritage can be preserved and India's linguistic diversity can become a cause of national pride. To return to Mahasweta's story, the question it raises is, must every elephant cease to be?

The Clash of Human Visions of Reality

THE INCREASED FREQUENCY WITH WHICH COMMENTS ON gods have resulted in hurt sensibility and uncontrolled anger makes one probe the exact nature of the attachment that human society has to the idea of divinity in a human-like form. Any speculation on when in prehistory and how precisely the idea of god emerged would be futile, since we do not have any definite details about the underlying social or psychological processes. For instance, we do not know if the Neanderthal or the *Homo erectus* had any idea of gods and if yes, whether these ideas were identical. In the case of *Homo sapiens* too, the idea may have emerged at a much later stage in their advent towards building civilisations. No other animal species have prayer practices and worship icons. It is likely that gods got conceptualised after humans accepted to cover their bodies, not just for protection from cold but also out of a sense of shame of nudity. The emergence of what psychology describes as 'alterity', the sense of 'otherness' is associated with the sense of shame experienced by individuals. It is the same instinctive alterity that makes one conceptualise another being, a far more powerful other who controls the world.

Acquisition of language, some seventy thousand years ago, helped humans articulate the imagination of a larger energy or being. This initial form of realisation of a larger power acquired the rudimentary form of collective offerings or prayers only after humans started forming society, each such social formation distinctly differing from others. In short, the idea of 'god' required a social identity accepted by its members, a society that collectively placed the responsibility of creation on an agency that was larger than and prior to humans. Since no one knew through direct experience what that unnamed agency was, it was imagined to be beyond birth, and possibly beyond death. It got described as being created by itself, 'omnipotent' and 'omnipresent'. Additionally, since it was not bound by material laws, it was also seen as entirely transcendental.

The 'all pervading, all present, all creating' idea of such an agency, shared by a large number of individuals in a given prehistoric or ancient society became 'god'. By then, humans had moved quite a long way from their pre-human and animal-like condition. They had figured out how to have clothing, dwelling and survival ability. They had already gathered a substantial experience of material things, what today we call the 'laws of physics'. Their imagination of 'God', therefore, took the form of a craving for a domain of being/existence that was entirely free of the material, mortal world of humans. All earliest descriptions of God or gods invariably invoked the non-material aspects of their being. The transcendental was free of the constraints of the real or what Immanuel Kant termed the 'phenomenal'. Human societies have moved ahead in history over the last few millennia, trying to accommodate in their mental transactions the phenomenal as well as the transcendental as two aspects of their being and becoming. The sects that emerged over time, the godheads that came to be worshipped, the prophets claiming to represent divinity who founded various religions, despite their differences, have all attempted to build bridges between the two world views.

Over the last few centuries, the advancement of thought, often propelled by the contradiction between the clergy class and the ideation of the 'omniscient' principle, has brought humans closer to proposing and generating a third kind of reality. At this juncture, we call it the virtual reality. In this domain of the virtual, space and time do not hinder movements of its inhabitant. The laws of motion and matter applicable in the phenomenal world pose no constraints to possibilities unfolded by the virtual world. Just as in the past, where the conceptualisation of the transcendental attracted societies to attempt entering the transcendental, through intuition, imagination, aspiration or at worst through blind ritualistic imitation, in the present, humans are attracted to the idea of entering the virtual. No individual, no field of knowledge, no society, no area of action and no state has remained untouched by the mesmerising attraction for the virtual. In the past, any degree of closeness to the transcendental was interpreted as ethically desirable; in our time, any degree of inwardness to the virtual is seen as a new mix of knowledge and power. If the invention of language and its advancement to a new order of complexity was the foundation of the transcendental, the invention of a new and a complex order of silence—call it aphasia—is expected to provide the foundation for the virtual in the future. Memory chips and digits are its building blocks, and cyborgs its inhabitants. It shall not occupy any space in the phenomenal world. It shall not work within the laws of temporality surrounding human life, thought and action. Yet, it is not just another version of the transcendental. The transcendental was believed to know 'all', including its beginning and its end, though humans were not privy to that knowledge. The memory chips, on the other hand, shall not know how or from where they came.

Caught in the tripartite visions of 'reality'—the phenomenal, the transcendental and the virtual—human societies are in a tangle that has no precedence in the entire history of man's evolution. The inexorable and speedy drift of everyone in the direction of the virtual, irrespective of economic class, gender, ethnicity, language, theological affiliation and nationality, has posed a vastly profound challenge to both the transcendental as well as the phenomenal view of reality. The heightened sensitivity to gods and God-related matters is a symptom of that stress. It has also placed tremendous stress on the phenomenal view of reality. The rather surprising eruption of ultra-sensitive nationalism at the beginning of a century initially lauded as the 'knowledge century' points to that anxiety. In the process of evolution, the formations and features that were nearing their end have been known in the past to have briefly bounced with ferocity and rage before they were discarded. If one were to think, without losing one's temper, and with a philosophical inwardness, it appears that the ideas of hyper-nationalism as well as hyper-sensitive attachment to any religion are doomed to be submerged in the avalanche of the virtual that is rapidly taking over the human world. The idea of a Hindu nation and an Islamic state has one thing in common—they cannot survive for long given the new turn that the human vision of reality has taken.

Living in Two Worlds

IF ONE WERE TO THINK OF A SINGLE ICONIC SCHOLAR OF Indian culture from the last century and half, the name of Ananda Kentish Coomaraswamy easily comes to mind. Going by the restrictive definition of who is an Indian, A.K. Coomaraswamy does not stand to qualify. Like Verrier Elwin, born in England and working in India for over four decades, AKC was born in England to a Ceylonese father and an English mother. He came to India only because Ceylon (currently Sri Lanka) had very close ties with India during the British era. He went on to make Buddhism and Hindu philosophy his areas of study, studied and collected vast amounts of information on all forms of Indian art and wrote copiously about them. If anything, it is his writings that make him 'Indian'. He engaged with the greatest minds of his time—Tagore and Gandhi—and was deeply involved in the philosophies of various civilisations and eras. His deep learning is reflected in every piece he wrote on Indian culture, making him as one of the greatest commentators of the essential India. The most widely read among his works was *The Dance of Siva*. The cover of the book, based on a key essay in it, shows the image of Nateswara (also known popularly as Nataraja or Ardha-Nari-Nateswara). The image, a pictorial representation of an ancient icon sculpted with amazing precision and grace, combining feminine delicacy and masculine vigour, is a great symbol that represents our civilisation.

The combination of the feminine and the masculine has fascinated Indian imagination for as long as India has been a civilisation. In the story of the Mahabharata, the most valorous warrior among the Pandavas—Arjuna—takes the role, for a short period, of Brihannada, a dancing girl. And, indeed, standing in the middle of the warring armies, he tells Sri Krishna that he is assailed at that very moment by signs of *'klaibya'* (loss of manliness)—*'sidanti mam gatrani, mukhamchya parishusyatih'* ('my mouth has gone dry, my limbs are trembling'). It is this condition of Arjuna that, Krishna tells him, makes him fit to gain the *divya-chakshu* (the divine eye), enabling him to understand the essence of life and death. The story of Shikhandi, who manages to cause Bhishma's death, is also well known.

One gets the optics of union between the feminine and the masculine countless times throughout India's cultural history. Two outstanding examples are Kabir in the medieval times and the nineteenth-century Bengali saint Ramakrishna Paramhans. Ashis Nandy, in his brilliant analysis of India's resistance to colonialism, explains how Mahatma Gandhi combined the feminine and the masculine in his actions and appearance, and emerged in Indian consciousness as an icon of resistance to the British. Seen from the Freudian perspective, the salt satyagraha, *'mauna'* or silence and non-cooperation were, in Nandy's view, typically feminine methods of resistance. In any case, it is true that Gandhi's satyagraha became an effective political instrument only after Kasturba joined him in the long march in South Africa. Shyam Benegal's film *The Making of Mahatma*, which depicts Gandhi's life in South Africa, accurately captures the gender transformation in Gandhi's politics between 1910 and 1915.

It is not just in myth, art or mysticism that the dualities are sought to be dissolved in India. The world view and narratives of material existence too show a co-mingling of dualities. The Greek mythology had in its early phase stories about gods and humans exchanging sentiments and aspirations, often creating a clash between the two realms of existence. But later, Greek mythology gave way to physics and philosophy, leading to a rupture between the realm of human affairs and the realm of the superhuman. The notion of an 'idea' or 'ideal' — as understood by Greeks — was born in the belief, or rather, the fear, that the world of ideas and the world of humans cannot be reconciled. Here it must be remembered that 'idea' did not mean for them 'a concept or a thought', but a kind of a 'thing or an existence' that has a perennial and non-diminishing life in the realm of the supernatural. The impossibility of reconciliation between ideas and objects pushed Greek thinkers towards grounding every branch of knowledge in fundamental binaries. Their thought got forever caught in antonyms, and in the tension arising out of their differences.

Indian traditions of philosophy did not hit that point of disillusionment with dualities. They continued believing in the permeability of the two. Possibilities of exchange, cross-migration and the belief that the two realms remain interchangeable became the core of thought traditions and life objectives in India. Call it, if you like, a mix-up theology. One terrible result of the mix-up theology was that the idea of re-birth came to settle in Indian thought and life; and irrespective of any change in the material culture of the people, it has sustained. Another result is the naive belief that 'traditions' continue to be accessible even when one has entered deep inside 'modernity'. The third major consequence is that people carry out their material and worldly life along one track of assumptions and beliefs while holding on to another set of diametrically opposed beliefs as 'values'.

In a book written by an Englishman in the 1920s—having read it nearly fifty years ago, I can remember neither the author nor the title—the author expresses a sense of bemusement to see professors of physics in Pune's Fergusson College teaching Western science to their students in the morning, and then moving onto a Satyanarayan Katha in the evening. Asked if the two do not clash in their thoughts, they were surprised, and responded, 'But why? This is how we are.' Back in 2023, I was having a serious conversation with a group of biologists in an elite research institution in Bangalore. This was soon after the NCERT had decided to throw Darwin out of India's school textbooks. One of the scientists I was talking to had been the head of a very large science research centre. When I asked them if there was no clash in their minds between Darwin's idea of evolution and the ancient Indian texts considered 'sacred', they frankly answered in the negative. Some of them had not thought about it. Those who had, explained that it was possible for them to keep the two arenas separate in their thought processes without minimising the importance of either.

James Joyce's *A Portrait of the Artist as a Young Man* is a classic of Western literature, depicting the agonising conflict between Church ethics and artistic freedom. That agony does not assail Indian minds when they confront such profound dualities. Eight decades ago, the Indian novelist Raja Rao wrote a brilliant narrative depicting a Nambudri Brahmin who turned to Marxist politics. Titled *Comrade Kirillov*, the novel has a protagonist who knows every verse of both Shankara's *Bramhasutrabhashya* and every word of Marx's *Das Capital*. He can comment on both with utmost brilliance, and defend every phrase in the two texts. That is India, perhaps.

Ashis Nandy, mentioned earlier, has argued that the moral ambivalence and gender mix in the minds of Indians has been one of the methods of resistance in the Indian past. He mentions other methods of resistance too, which include Buddhism and Bhakti (as in the Bhakti literature of medieval India). But, he argues, androgyny and ambivalence excel all other methods of resistance in Indian history. I tend to agree with him.

All of this discussion of India's cultural and philosophic peculiarities is of particular importance today. The current regime, driven by Savarkar's understanding of the Indian past and the RSS's understanding of Indian society, is busy militarising Hinduism. That, in fact, was one of the prescriptions suggested by Savarkar in *The Essentials of Hindutva*. The regime, however, despite its decisive majority in the Parliament, its electoral success and its money and muscle power, has not fully grasped how Indians react to political phenomena. In the Karnataka elections, neither the chest-thumping masculinity nor the polarisation of voters managed to deliver the expected results for the BJP. In Manipur, women power has reduced state power to a nought. Similarly, the 'labharthis'—a new term popularised by the BJP for 'the obliged beneficiaries of government schemes'—have not been as obliging in panchayat elections in most states. The fact that despite massive job losses and unbearable price hike, Indian citizens have not followed the example of their Sri Lankan counterparts in their response to massive rise in petrol prices, is taken by the regime as an indication of Narendra Modi's popularity. Quite likely, it is a gross misreading of the apparent silence of the masses. Coomaraswamy describes in his essay on Siva's dance the mythical Tandava, a dance of wrath arising out of an enigmatic silence. In future, we will know if India's cultural grounding prevails or if the regime has managed to bring about a complete metamorphosis.

A Song for India

If music be the food of love, play on,
Give me excess of it that, surfeiting,
The appetite may sicken and so die.
That strain again, it had a dying fall.
O, it came o'er my ear like the sweet sound
That breathes upon a bank of violets,
Stealing and giving odour. Enough, no more,
'Tis not so sweet now as it was before.

THESE ARE THE IMMORTAL LINES WITH WHICH SHAKESPEARE'S romantic play *The Twelfth Night* opens. Indeed, music is the food for love; and indeed, too much of it—music or love—may induce nausea. I am invariably reminded of these lines every time I get caught in the singing orgy called 'antakadi' (in Hindi). The Gujarati word for this 'sport' is 'antakshari' and the Marathi word is 'bhendya'. For a long time, I was under the impression that this rather strange group music-sport is confined to the western and northern parts of India. But as I travelled to other parts of India, I realised I was wrong. The rules of the game are as simple as they can be. One fellow sings a couple of lines of some popular song, never mind how terribly rendered. What matters is the last syllable of the last line. The opposing team has to pick up from there and sing anything that begins with that syllable. Once this is done, the first group sings yet another song beginning with the terminal syllable of the song sung by the opponents. Any person from the group can sing. All that this sport needs is two groups and plenty of free time. I have noticed that when school children go for long tours, they resort to this game to reduce the boredom of the long bus journey or train travel. I have not seen school children or college children in European or North American countries doing this. It is a peculiarly Indian phenomenon. I am inclined to believe that this is prevalent in African countries too; but I can say it with no surety. One aspect of the game that may interest ethnographers and psychologists is that even girls and boys who are shy when left to their individual self and have hesitation in conversing or mixing with the opposite sex, tend to let go of their shyness when they join the 'antakadi' groups. This musical pastime play enables the release of suppressed desires, exactly as smearing strangers with colours, with no gender distinction, does during the festival of Holi. In that sense, the antakadi is a ritual created by a repressed society that helps adolescent persons gain an outlet for their concealed attraction for the other sex. But is there something more to the shrill songs of the bored young travellers than the mere ritual of widening intimacy with the opposite gender?

I saw this question in a very different light when I started working with Adivasis. During the 1990s, I used to track migrant Adivasi labourers. They used to walk long distances, over a hundred kilometres in some cases, and settled on make-shift camps in cities for the duration they worked on construction sites. I noticed that in evenings, women often got together and sang. It was not unusual for men too to join them. Those were the songs they had carried from their villages, which had been inherited by their elders from their ancestors. Back in their villages, I noticed that they sang when they sowed the fields in monsoon. They also sang songs after burying their dead. In short, they had songs for all seasons, all occasions! Those songs kept them rooted to their families, their villages and their past. It was as if music was a different kind of language, not a language that names, describes and analyses the world, but a language that connects, internalises and remembers.

In India, one is a social member either of a tribe or a caste. Thinking of tribal songs, my mind went back to the wedding songs that I had heard sung by elder women in my community. I normally avoid attending weddings; but I am aware that in most communities, there are songs related to various wedding rituals. There are songs to bid goodbye to the brides going off to their in-laws, and songs that welcome them at the in-laws. There are songs to be sung when women become pregnant and songs when the child is born and given a name. These songs of arrivals and departures provide a sense of continuity. In winter, after the Indian countryside gets close to the cropping season, songs waft in the air from a distance at night, invariably accompanied by drum and harmonium. If you walk up to the singing group, you notice that those are songs drawn from medieval saints—Kabir, Meera, Tukaram, Akka Mahadevi, Narsinh Mehta Thyagraj and so many others. Those songs have been in the air for centuries now. Their charm has not worn out; their soul-stirring appeal has not dulled.

Every time I travel abroad, I miss the songs of India. Of course, there are nightclubs and there is music of a different kind. Yet, the song that wells up from the heart and brings back the deep memory of the distant past, the song that makes you meditative, is not to be found. I have noticed that the range of songs that an Indian knows—film songs, folk songs, qawwalis, powadas or bhajans—is much larger than what the folks in Europe and America know. Formal music is one thing. Music scores written by great composers is without a doubt worthy of adoration. Bands playing their own compositions are admirable too. Yet, they are not quite the same as the free-flowing songs that belong to everyone—the unwritten, non-formal music. The engagement of the Indian consciousness with this vast ocean of songs and its informal and unorganised transfer from one generation to another is almost the defining attribute of India as a civilisation. This, and not so much the great philosophies and darshanas, emperors and heroes, is at the heart of Indian culture. We are many languages, many histories, many people; but we are united in our deep relation with the songs of India. I imagine Bharat-mata as a rich, prolific and free-flowing musical presence.

In recent years, one notices a new cultural war waged in the Indian society which may leave India altered forever. But since the cultural warriors have not been able to bring in any new music, any great songs to India, will they be able to win the heart of India? The British rule contributed to many areas of life in India, but not so much to its songs. When it ended, it ended forever. In contrast, the Persian rulers of India brought in with them glorious traditions of music; and their presence continues to manifest itself through the many cultural traditions of India. In time, the ideology that dominates the public discourse may go into oblivion; but will it have left any cultural mark, except memories of avoidable violence and hatred? For, indeed, music is the food of love.

Contrarian Present and the Human Future

In November 2019, I was at the Raman Physics Institute in Bangalore for a lecture. A group of scientists there have been carrying out a mapping of the cosmos not yet known to us. This involves, literally, keeping an eye on cosmic events and material dynamics in that unimaginably vast space, if space indeed is as we understand it. Listening to their reports on the billions of galaxies and dark matters beyond the ken of present human knowledge made me think, once again, how minuscule a speck of matter our earth is in the cosmic scheme of things. It also made me think if 'life', its evolution on earth over the last 2.5 billion years, and if human intelligence has any role to play in the infinite cosmic space and time. The quest for unravelling the unknown has attracted the human mind for millennia, and our various triumphs along the way are worthy of taking pride in.

Just as the quest for the unknown is propelling current research, so is the fear of the unknown. On 28 November

2019, Damian Carrington, the environment editor of *The Guardian*, published a definitive report stating that the scientific community around the world has more or less concluded that we are now well past the 'tipping points' of environmental disaster. Quoting scientists from several important universities, the report lists the melting of ice in the Antarctic and the Arctic, pumping a vast amount of CO_2 into the atmosphere, exposing life on earth to unbearable levels of radiation, and increase in the global temperatures by several degrees. The Carrington report argues that even an increase of 1 degree centigrade in the arctic temperature would be enough for the oceans to wash away innumerable cities and towns located on sea coasts. The higher tidal waves will not be able to differentiate cities by their names such as Kolkata, Mumbai, New York or Perth when they hit the coastline in fury.

Environmental degradation is no longer just a new finding in science research. In several states, the monsoons now unleash a fury unlike anything experienced in the past several decades. In Maharashtra alone, the damage caused to agriculture due to the floods is so enormous that no amount of compensation can meet even 4 per cent of the loss incurred by farmers. Millions of agrarian families have faced the brunt and they may take at least a decade to recover from its effects. Sudden floods and unexpected droughts have by now become a common occurrence not just in Maharashtra but all states. So is the suffocating air quality experienced by Delhi year after year. Typhoons, tornadoes, cloudbursts and tsunamis too have become more frequent than before. Add to this the forest fires in America and Australia, scorching summers in Europe, bitter winters in many continents and the general unpredictability of weather in all parts of the world. Going by these signs, it is certain that humans have played havoc with air and water, the two non-negotiable requirements for continuation of life—not just human life, but all forms of life.

The sharp contrast between man's cosmic quest and the neglect of the earth is not the only one that characterises our time. Ever since man put wheels to the service of his desire to spread out and conquer distance, the craving for increased velocity has dominated our material development. The notion of 'escape velocity', which will permit flying objects to overcome the earth's gravitational pull, is by now a settled idea. Attaining that speed will allow earthbound humans to step into a world that has no constraints, either of space or of time. Yet, while speed technologies and space science have already enabled humans to accomplish escape velocity, the forward movement of many countries appears to have suddenly taken a U-turn. After a continuous march of the idea of democracy towards humanitarian political order, we are now witnessing the collapse of public institutions that form the very pillars of democracy. This situation prevails not just in India, but even in countries that were considered, until recently, the role models for democratic political systems and liberal society. The decline of progressive and liberal parties and their electoral defeat in country after country have not yet been fully analysed, but the fact that the decline is no fluke is fully accepted by analysts in all countries. The dominance of the extreme conservatives and the ultra-right, consciously mounting an attack on institutions cherished by the left-liberals, drawing societies back to the semi-medieval mood of narrow nationalism, hatred and violence, stands in sharp contrast to man's desire to attain full escape velocity which in turn would take us to a never-before imagined arena of freedom.

There is one more eye-catching and quite puzzling context that marks our time. Recently, the champion Korean player of the traditional Chinese game 'Go' decided to retire as, according to his testimony, he thought it impossible for him to beat the artificial intelligence (AI) pitted against him in the game. For the last two centuries, humans have longed to create intelligent machines and have spawned quite an array of them, making our jobs easier in almost all fields of life. The fascinating developments in robotics and AI in recent decades make humans look almost like the creator of the universe; and, yet the very same triumph is now turning out to be the beginning of the endgame.

Closer to our everyday lives, the same contrast can be seen in man's arrival at economies of surplus that are burdened by worry related to job losses, slowdown, depression, and collapse of industry and enterprise. Closer to us, again, in the year of remembering the greatest apostle of truth in history, our public discourse is assailed by post-truth. Similarly, in the times of the vast spread of communication, the media all over the world has become almost empty of meaningful content. Whether it is close to our rushed everyday life or in sanitised scientific laboratories away from us, we seem to be caught in a series of paradoxes difficult to explain with traditional logic and nearly impossible to reconcile. The anxiety caused by the breakdown of dialogue between the irreconcilable contraries marks the mood for our times.

In human history, whenever a clash of ideas and a breakdown of dialogue has set in, human advent has come to a standstill. But history shows that such times are also when new and powerful ideas are in the offing. Almost as a result of the clash of contraries, new norms for the society spring up, as the poet Shelly said, 'like a child from a womb, like a ghost from a tomb, and unbuild the dome of the sky again', giving birth to a new world. Surely then, the human species is at the threshold of a new age that shall have little to do with what constituted normal in the past or present—in politics, economies, thought and culture. Going by the story of the human advent so far, we are enveloped at present in a silence before the proverbial outbreak of a storm. Perhaps not all is lost; perhaps, the future can still be ours.

Towards 2047

NEARING THE END OF THE FIRST QUARTER OF THE TWENTY-first century, we are burdened with responsibilities that have had no match in its seriousness since Independence. Our path to the future on the horizon of 2047 is strewn with challenges. In the near and distant future, there are unprecedented struggles waiting for us. We are now a nation with a population of 1.4 billion. To start off, we have the great task of cleansing the minds of people of the poison of communal hatred. We have to bring in governments that are sensitive to people's needs and perceptions, strive to give our federal structure the centrality it deserves and safeguard India as a plural and diverse society. We have to work towards restoring the institutions that secure democratic checks and balances in the system and ensure that the media regains its freedom and self-confidence. We have to make education and basic healthcare accessible to everyone as a fundamental right and ensure equitable livelihood opportunities to those whose economic condition calls for rescue. Most of all, letting women exercise the rights that legitimately belong to them and ensuring dignity to Adivasis and DNTs is an obligation that needs be fulfilled. Protection of the nation's natural environment and safeguarding ecological balance are issues that demand serious attention. Protecting individual privacy and dignity in the face of the advent of artificial memory and artificial intelligence (AI) is also as daunting a challenge. All these call for deep reflection on who we are, where we are and, indeed, what we will be in 2047.

The beginning of the year 2000 had brought great excitement among people all over the world. It was the year marking the beginning, not just of a new century, but a new millennium. Many names were suggested as historical tags for the new century; but probably the one that was received with the greatest enthusiasm was 'knowledge century'. Two and a half decades may not be a long span of time; but time, indeed, has humbled humans, for no one uses the term today to refer to our present times. The world has meekly accepted to look askance at what is in store for *homo sapiens*. At this juncture, the future looks embattled, surrounded by newly unfolding war fronts.

In 2020, news reports about a strange war made rounds in several newspapers in Karnataka. These reports covered an on-going war between elephants and humans. Some eight hundred elephants roaming in what is known as the 'elephant corridor' of the Western Ghats have opened a systematic war with the human habitants there. It is being recorded by the forest officials since 2014. During the course of it, many humans have been maimed by elephants and so many elephants have been shot dead. The tension between the two warring sides is so acute that the forest officials in the Hassan district have decided to install censors to alert the inhabitants to the presence of elephants in the vicinity. Just a month before this story came to the limelight, there were reports about the outburst of bush-forest fires in Australia. The geographic spread and the frequency with which those fires erupted were mind-boggling. They spread over nearly 1,10,000 sq. km and had, in a single week, caused the death of thirty-three persons. The sheer number of trees destroyed by these wanton fires runs into millions. Australia is not the only continent where forest fires have besieged humans. The North and South Americas, East Africa and Southeast Asia have also witnessed increase in the frequency with which forests are getting gulped by uncontrollable wild fires. Rarely does a week pass without the news of a forest fire in some part of the world. Needless to say, scientists have clearly come to the conclusion that the transition of humanity from the Holocene to the Anthropocene is irreversible.

When I mention the difficulties and the distance separating us from the horizon of 2047, my mind goes back to the years 1920-21. I try to think how Indians back then would have imagined 1947 to be, a time when India would gain its Independence, although they could not have anticipated a specific date back then. I can think of two defining moments of 1921. One is the launch of Dr Ambedkar's *Mook-nayak*, the origin of all rights-based movements for Indian society since then. The second, equally or even more momentous was the complete sartorial transformation of barrister Gandhi in the September of 1921 and his becoming the president of the Congress in December that year. Though independence was still twenty-six years away, their actions held within them the promise of a new dawn. I am not trying to minimise the significance of our epic freedom struggle in which thousands became martyrs and millions contributed in their own way. All that I am trying to suggest is that gaining freedom and an inclusive constitution became possible because the thought in that direction had already sprouted and was clearly visible in 1921. In order to grasp 2047 in our view, we similarly need a better grasp of the nature of the struggle ahead of us. In it, if I may so propose, the foremost will be our ability to grasp that the existence and survival of humans are governed by the ecology within which the *homo sapiens* thrive. Similarly, we need to grasp how deep we have arrived inside the virtual world peopled by AI and artificial memory. I shall comment here at some length on one of the two conditions that will characterise us in 2047.

Political scientists all over the world are seriously worried about the future of democracy, at least the kind of democracy the world had envisioned during the twentieth century. Among the more conventional threats to the safe continuation of democracy such as illiteracy, corruption, nepotism and bigotry is now added a far more serious threat coming from the emergence of AI, control of masses by machines, use of spyware and assault on individual privacy.

The idea of democracy took birth in the desire to rebel against the idea of '*That*', '*It*', 'the pastness beyond past', the Upanishidic '*tat*', or anything that was outside the reach of man's rational abilities. Though the specific historical particulars differ from nation to nation, the desire to adopt democracy as the form of government has a shared universal narrative. It is a relatively new social and political arrangement which is bound to have an uneasy relationship with a mystified and deified past. Besides, the historical moment of arrival of democracy as an arrangement of power, which coincided with the birth of rationality as the foundation of science and modernity as an ecosystem of sensibility, further strains the uneasy relationship between memory and democracy. For many centuries in the past, Utopia was seen as the mythical future. In the era of democracy, future ceases to be a mere myth and starts becoming the source of power, a function that memory had performed in pre-democratic ages. Democracy, with its attendant mental ecology of modernity and its uneasy relationship with the idea of the past, is struggling to deal with artificial memory. While it requires the future as a myth, it does not know how it can generate that myth in the time of artificial memory. This is going to be a long struggle and an entrenched debate that human societies will have to negotiate in the decades to come. Meanwhile, artificial memory, which is neither capable of generating myth nor giving birth to dreams, can only produce rumours, illusions, hypnotising chimera or mesmerising terror. Short of dreams—as distinct from rumours and illusions—for the future, the democratic order will continue to limp forward unless humans seriously deliberate on the implications of the disjuncture between dreams and artificial memory.

At present, most governments in the world, including the Government of India, are busy using artificial memory to discipline, order and control citizens. In doing so, they are facilitating the primacy of artificial memory over democracy. The virtual world has posed a challenge to our established ideas of space and time. It provides legitimacy to non-matter as real and existent, while reducing the material into something that is incompletely existent. Citizens, therefore, cannot any longer be citizens unless they are in digital form, floating in virtual time and space. And, because they are substantially digital, the idea of equality seems no longer relevant to sizing them. It is, however, too late in history to think of knowledge and society without the obtrusive presence of artificial memory. In the twenty-first century, democracy can redeem itself neither by seeking to extend the grip of technology over psychology, nor by calling to aid the 'inner strength' of democracy. That has already faded out a few decades ago, not just in India but in most other countries.

Democracy can and, one hopes, *will*, redeem itself not by an obsolete mystification of history and memory. It can be redeemed by grasping the absolute contradiction between natural memory and artificial memory. Politics that is obsessively interested in making the imagined glorious past its sole plank is quite hopelessly out of tune with the historical shifts in the trajectory of memory and its impact on the forms of government. Similarly, politics which is entirely technology-driven has a view of the future that can only hasten the decline of democracy. In the twenty-first century, pro-democratic politics will have to make the gods and robots confront each other in order to rebuild the future as a myth and invent artificial memory that is capable of a sense of its past. They need to meet and transform themselves to ensure that democracy continues to thrive. What India will be in 2047 depends on how efficiently we get into the man–machine tangle and spell out the charter of rights, dignity and privacy once again in view of the newly emerged complexities, so that we do not have a new constitution beginning with the sentence, 'We, the digitally numbered and the Robots of India, hereby adopt, enact and give to ourselves, ...' Let us pray that the angry, winged sea horse of Greek mythology, Pegasus, does not scorch our democracy, won through the sacrifice of life by real humans in the real world.

I will now turn to the real people in the real world. The year 2021 marked the 150th year of Lord Mayo's enactment of the 1971 Criminal Tribes Act. The Act put several hundred helpless communities under the stigma of 'criminality'. They were detained in reformatory settlements well until 1952, when the CTA was 'de-notified' and they became the denotified communities, yet remained stigmatised. The Republic has not bothered to think of them in its plans, policies or provisions. The fate of the Adivasis is similar to that of the DNTs. They have been asking for the legitimate ownership of land, their *pattas*. In their case, despite provisions, plans and policies, the *patta* still eludes their grasp. If they raise their voice, they are treated as Naxalites. If you sympathise with them, you are branded as 'urban Naxalites'. This, when the Australian government tendered an unconditional apology to the aborigines of Australia long back, and the UN decided to come up with its *Indigenous Peoples Declaration*.

Despite the mobilisation resulting from Dr Ambedkar's heroic efforts, the scheduled castes of India, in recent years, have seen more mob lynching instances than the Black did in the USA during the pre-Lincoln era. And, alas, we now live in times when every child associates Islam with terrorism. The Indian society has always been fragmented in the past. But where it stands today, its fissures and fragmentation far surpass all instances in the past. What is worse is that the political and social activism energy necessary to bring people together lack a complete grasp of the nature of the problem. Please allow me to propose that no longer can we bring people together merely by reading to each other the Upanishads, the Quran and Bible, for our ideas of social segments and social classes have come under the influence of a deterministic view of people. Political energy applied in the past by visionary thinkers and mass leaders to bring citizens within a single matrix of class, race and gender is not compatible with a society which refuses to understand *difference* because though it exists materially, it disappears from view in the digital realm. For acquiring this ability, we need a transformative political energy.

The visions we see as transformative today are bogged down with a burden of dry numbers, data-sheets, graphs and a narrative related to numbered bodies. There is no space for views and perspective that measure distance comparatively and progress in terms of local and personal aspirations. Identity politics rooted in demonising the 'others', therefore, can no longer be the driving engine for any movement that seeks to transcend the narrowness of identities. The society depicted in digits fails to grasp what is narrow and what is not. Nation, in its earliest form, was the people. Nation, in its subsequent ideological forms, became the past of a people and the future of the people. The past imagined as being spread over a very long span of time becomes a challenge to memory and begins acquiring the form of myth, which is irrationally compressed and imaginatively transformed over time. The future, as against the past, spread over an endless time, becomes a challenge to the imagination and acquires the form of fantasy or utopia, albeit compressed, and fantasy driven re-statements of the idea of time. Therefore, a nation can live in real time only when it has a range of myths recognised by the people as their own and a fantasy or utopia owned by the people as of their own making.

The widening middle class in India is not entirely a product of the increase in income levels of its citizens. It is also in a large measure the result of the food sufficiency and textile sufficiency that India was able to attain. It created a population not exactly rich, but at the same time not exactly poor, resembling middle classes elsewhere, yet not quite the middle class as seen through the lens of social analysts. The upper layer in the wide spectrum of the 'middle' class in India is not given to overstatement of its religious identity, though it is deeply attached to various theological sects and practices. The lower section of the 'middle' class is indeed ready to place theological identity among its ways and means of attaining prosperity. Science, but mainly technology, and material wealth are the primary interests of the upper layer. Therefore, they feel easily attracted to the neoliberal economic order and the benefits it brings to them. The lower middle class is interested in the public affirmation of theological identity in order to achieve upgradation in the social hierarchy (referred to as Sanskritisation) and the potential benefits it may bring to them in the future. Any political formation keeping the middle class in focus involves the risk of generating, in the long run, a clash between science and technology on the one hand and identity and theology on the other. This cannot be avoided if politics continues to be shaped by the perspective of the right wing, middle-class majoritarian rule.

In thinking of India, one is thinking of all people, all cultures, all languages, all religions and all diversities with which India is blessed. Fortunately, we are a federation. Federalism is a natural consequence if nature has brought together vast territories and kept them together through mutual interdependence. Federations born out of a gradually evolving entity can sustain itself, provided the sense of identity of its individual units is not overtly ethnic or linguistic. If identity acquires primacy, such a federation becomes less than convincing, as has happened in the case of the European Union. The Indian federation is not entirely territorial or natural. It is not the creature of a conquest. It is not as fragile as the European Union. What then is the catalyst for the federation that India is? Several waves of population settling down slowly over long stretches of history, and creating different languages in the process, is one pillar of the Indian federation. Immense geographical and climatic diversity causing the emergence of distinct cultural zones is the second pillar. Governments in India that ignore the historical and geographical context of India's formation can be detrimental to Indian federalism. In other words, when any Indian government attempts to overwhelm the Indian federation, India's federalism moves towards centripetal dynamics and the federation tends to turn fragile and shaky.

Cultural diversity, ecological diversity and linguistic diversity become less self-sure during a despotic regime. If the regime starts posing nationalism as an alternative to federalism, the unity of India comes under tremendous stress. Therefore, a totalitarian regime needs to be challenged, when such a need arises, by highlighting India's diversity, pluralism and its intrinsic federalism. At present, Indian federalism appears to be under severe strain. The pain caused by that is in all probability the birthplace of a new vision for India—a restorative, inclusive vision, that will allow for harmonious coexistence of diverse pluralities. Power, which constitutes the entire spectrum of the dominated and the dominators, requires, in order to be constituted in that manner, the consent of the dominated. As a scientific field of study, psychology looks at the desire to be dominated as well as the desire to dominate as mental abnormalities. Together, they form a continuum of illness. Were such an abnormality to become the norm itself, it would require a collective effort for its concealment so that no one calls it an abnormality. Various methods of concealing it used in the past and the present have taken the form of rituals. Every ritual associated with every form of domination is an attempt to conceal the widespread mental illness and turning the abnormality into a norm.

In a democracy, the representation of people is an ideal and a dream; but the processes formalised to actualise the ideal slip off the ideal. In course of time, the formalisation intended to articulate the ideal ends up as a ritual. As the gap between the ideal and the ritual increases, representation gets replaced by covert or overt domination. Primarily empty rituals replace the relation between the represented and those who are supposed to represent them. It may seem logical that if these rituals are unmasked, debunked and somehow made irrelevant, society can be pushed back to its original arrangement. However, that logic has a deep flaw in it; such an assault on rituals of representation may weaken those rituals as well as the ideal that they purport to embody. In the process, the idea of democracy itself may suffer a wound impossible to heal. The recovery of democracy is possible not by attacking the aberrations that have entered it but by reasserting the original idea.

Every manner of reassertion of democracy needs to question not how people are represented, but foregrounding what people want represented. Therefore, the business of the civil society should be not exposing the aberrations but restating the dream; not trying to clean the ground sullied by devious rituals but lifting the people's vision to newer and higher horizons of expectations. This task is very different from the task assigned by Karl Marx to the class capable of becoming society's critical consciousness. In fact, the task cannot be performed by a class; it can only be performed by individuals who refuse to belong to any class. The reinvention of democracy calls for public intellectuals who can place themselves outside class, race, gender and, most of all, the momentary rush of the events of the day.

The 1980s had brought to the world a fleeting vision of a one-world phase of the community of nations. Increased food sufficiency, better transport and oil tracking, more easily accessible healthcare and the promise of free flow of information formed the background of the German unification. In our country, those years were marked with the telecom and TV revolution. Despotic rules and dictatorships, where they existed, had started looking like expired ideas by mid-1980s. Liberal economic ideas were becoming ready to free the spirit of enterprise and creativity, and loosen the stifling regimes, making them supple and flexible. The fear of nuclear wars had started evaporating like a forgotten nightmare. The world imagined that the future wars would be fought against malnutrition, disease and illiteracy. International agencies were getting ready to spell out their agendas for programmes like the Millennium Development Goals and 'X for All'. However, over the last three decades, the mood has changed altogether, and as W.B. Yeats said a century ago, 'a terrible beauty is born'.

There is a cryptic definition of democracy which wits 'democracy is a rumour not as yet disproved'. In our time, it is indeed becoming a mere rumour—in Chile, Russia, USA, Nigeria, Egypt and even in our own country. During the last few years, there has been an inexplicable rise of anti-democratic sentiment all over the world. This is explained by left-leaning thinkers as the capture of the state by the corporate. Gandhians explain this as a predictable consequence of unchecked greed. The neoliberals explain this as a passing phase of the clash between technocratic ethics—'transparency' and 'fast-growth'—and the political order prone to 'populist' economic drives. There are also explanations stressing on the deviant personality traits of individuals, be it Donald Trump or Recep Erdogan. What is difficult to explain is, why so many of them and why all together? George Santayana had described his times as the world 'on a moral holiday'. Following him, one can probably say that the world today appears to be 'on a political holiday'. It is time for us to return from our political holiday, unmask the system, free it from the rituals that have replaced democracy and people's representation and face the challenges head on. It is time for us to understand that humans have to come to terms with AI on one hand, and with non-human life on our planet and beyond on the other. It is time for us to rethink and revitalise the idea of democracy as an integral part of the global, and even the cosmic, arrangement of life. Cosmo-democracy is the term being used for such an arrangement. It is time for us to think of rights beyond the rights just of the majority, of adults or of humans. We need to invent ways of respecting and protecting the rights of all marginal communities, all minorities, children and non-human life in the world known to us and in the worlds that may come to be in the near future, along with the rights of what is still not life—such as the AI—but is fast moving towards acquiring life.

What do these apparently diverse calamities threatening human existence indicate? Whether arising out of threats posed by microscopic viruses, radical environmental changes, AI, extra-terrestrial interference, sheer human arrogance towards nature, indifference to the suffering of fellow humans or insensitivity to the signs of degeneration, the nature of wars that humans have to fight in the near future will be unprecedented in history. The wars fought by us centuries ago, in the beginning of the second millennium, were mostly faith-based. They were crusades or jihads. The wars fought during the nineteenth century were nationalistic in character, based in ethnicity, language or contested territorial claims. The wars fought during the previous century were driven by ideologies combined with economic interests, whether they were wars caused by fascism, communism or capitalism. The wars waiting for us on the horizon are of a different character and order. These will be wars for or with the environment, with the forces of natural evolution, with non-human intelligence and with life and objects that belong to a different framework of matter and motion. Sadly, governments all over the world maintain an old-world mindset; they are prisoners of terribly dated political ideologies focused on faith-based divisions, territorial contestations and narrow nationalism. Though the proponents of cosmo-democracy have made a beginning by thinking about political systems necessary for equipping humans to fight these new wars, their voice is still very feeble and has reached only a very small circle of political scientists. But time is ticking fast. Shall we arrive there by 2047? Time alone will tell our future generations.